WITHDRAWN

WALLACE™ & GROMIT 2

Cracking Contraptions Manual

Illustrated by **Graham Bleathman**

Designed by **Lee Parsons**

Written by **Derek Smith**

Wallace & Gromit are characters created by Nick Park.

Published in October 2011

A catalogue record for this book is available from the British Library.

ISBN 978 0 85733 147 2

Haynes Publishing, Sparkford, Yeovil, Somerset BA22 7JJ, UK
Tel: +44 (0) 1963 442030 Fax: +44 (0) 1963 440001
E-mail: sales@haynes.co.uk
Website: www.haynes.co.uk

Haynes North America Inc.,
861 Lawrence Drive, Newbury Park,
California 91320, USA

Printed and bound by Wallace & Gromit.

AUTO LOCK

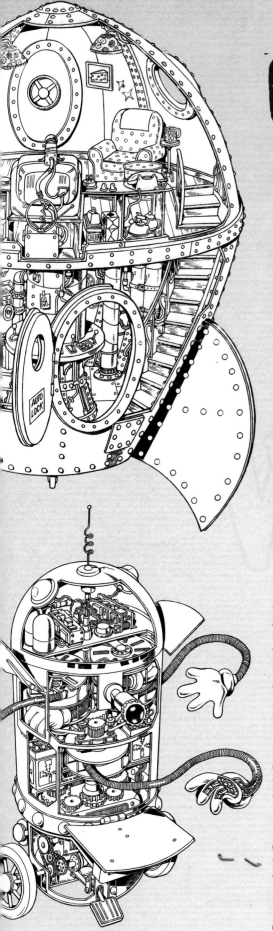

CONTENTS

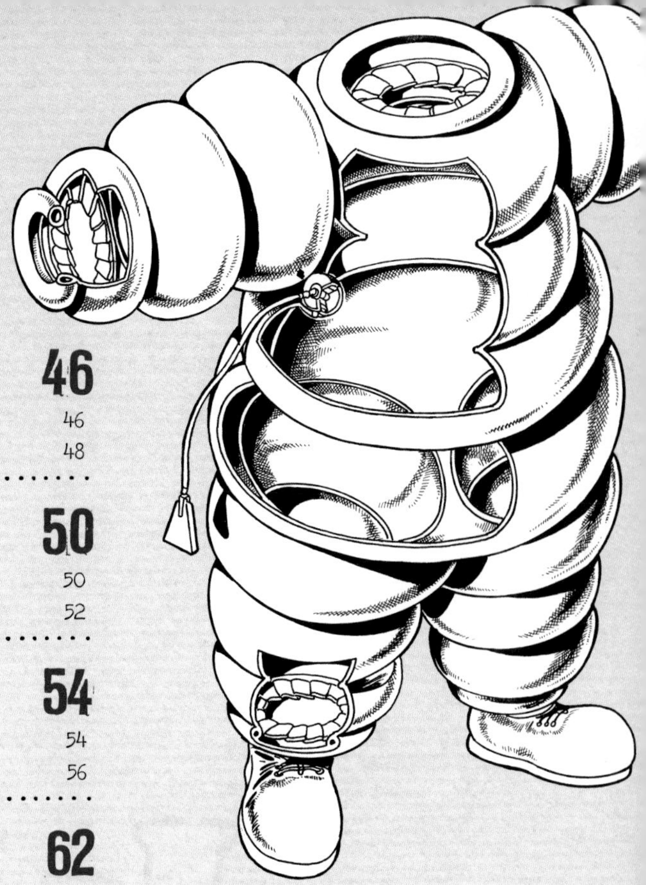

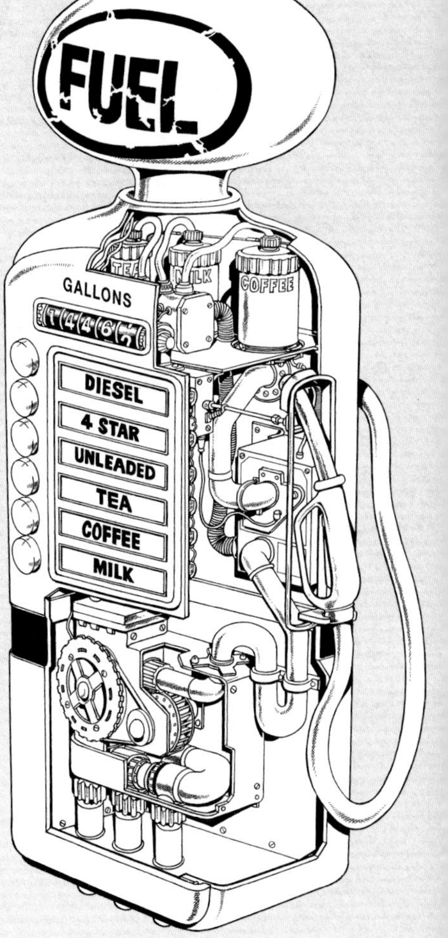

FUEL
GALLONS
COFFEE
DIESEL
4 STAR
UNLEADED
TEA
COFFEE
MILK

MAIN HEADING

(INTRODUCTION)
PRONTO PRINT

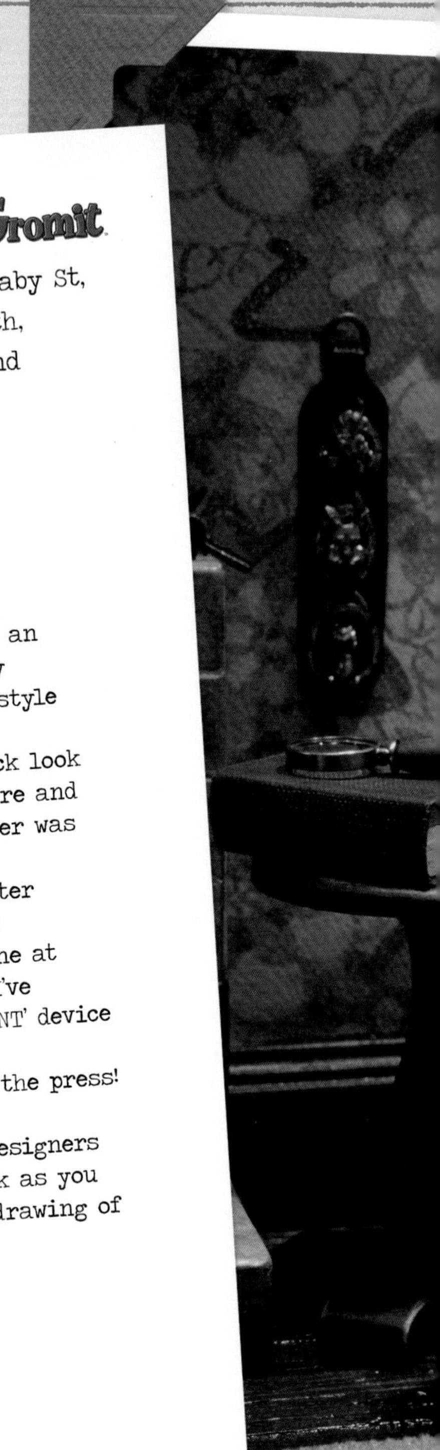

Wallace & Gromit

62 West Wallaby St,
Up North,
England

The Editor
Haynes Publishing Ltd
Sparkford
Somerset
BA22 7JJ

Dear Editor,

I'm so glad that everyone enjoyed the first book, and I have to agree it's an absolutely cracking idea to do a second one to show off a few more of my inventions. I'm sure readers who, like Gromit and me, enjoy a modern lifestyle will find plenty here to keep them occupied.

Once again your people have done us proud. Thank you. I've had a quick look through and, like last time, the text only needed the odd nip 'n' tuck here and there on every single page from 1 to 96 inclusively. The inside back cover was fine, by the way!

This time, however, I haven't sent back the proofs. This is because, after consulting with my constant canine companion, I've decided to try this publishing lark for myself. So you'll be delighted to know that everyone at Stains Manuals can now put their feet up and have a cuppa - because I've finished the book for you and printed it using my own new 'PRONTO PRINT' device (patent pending)!

In fact, you are holding in your hands the very first copy, hot off the press! (Please allow to cool before reading.)

Not only can Drains Publishing now do away with all its editors, designers and printers, but you can run off as many copies of the finished book as you need - at the push of a button! I've taken the liberty of including a drawing of my latest labour-saving device and a few notes on the next page.

So enjoy the book ... and thanks again!

Yours ever,

Wallace

Wallace

P.S. You can expect the first 50,000 copies sometime tomorrow afternoon. Will 3pm be ok - and is there parking for the van?

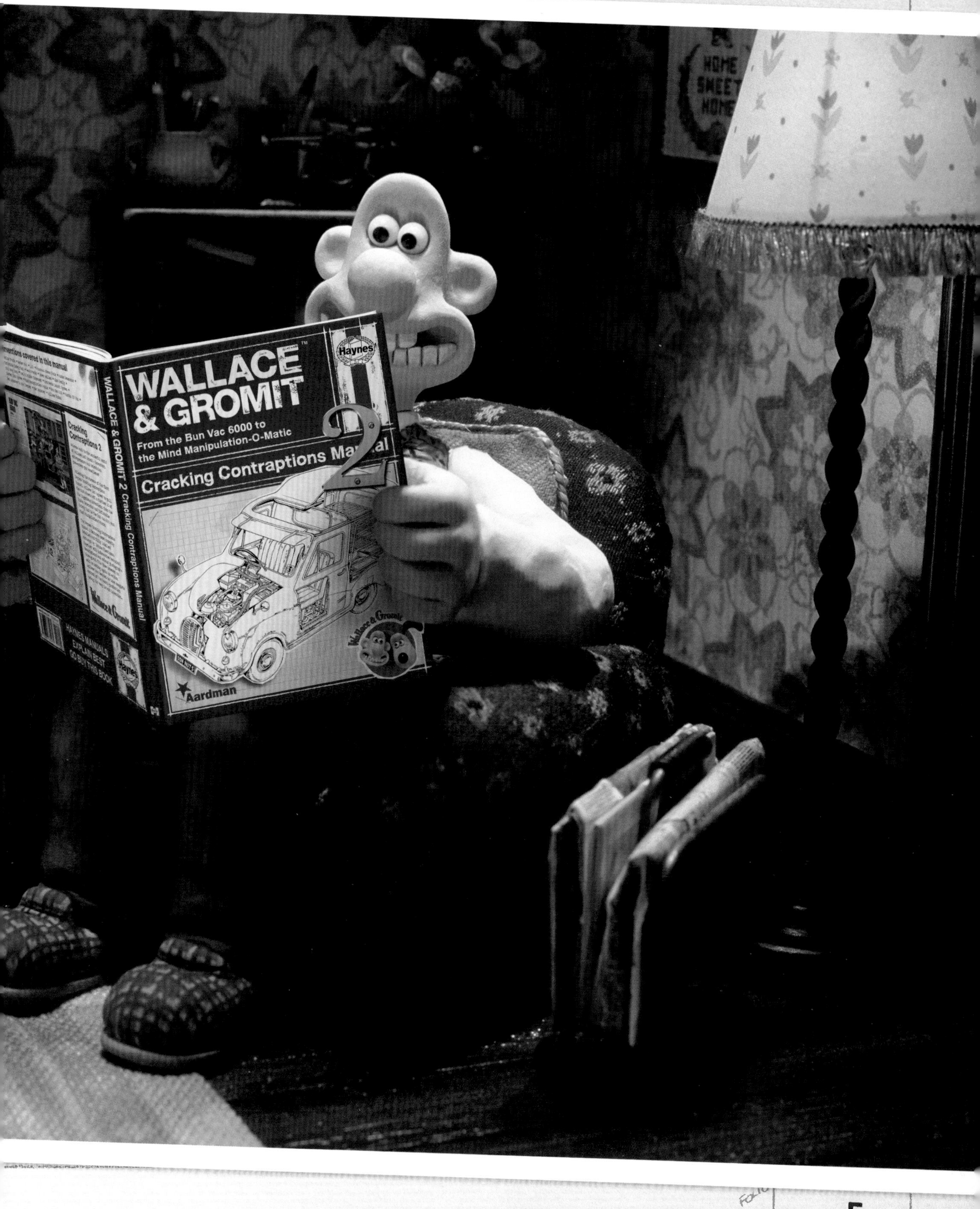
HOME SWEET HOME
Haynes
WALLACE & GROMIT
From the Bun Vac 6000 to the Mind Manipulation-O-Matic
2
Cracking Contraptions Manual
WALLACE & GROMIT 2 Cracking Contraptions Manual
Cracking Contraptions 2
HAYNES MANUALS EXPLAIN BEST GO BUY THIS BOOK
Aardman

SUB HEADING

Pronto Print

BULLET LIST

- ❶ Editor's chair.
- ❷ Manuscript holder.
- ❸ Text input keyboard.
- ❹ Printed text, ready for conveying to process camera.
- ❺ Editor's refreshments.
- ❻ Printed text is fed into process camera to finalise page layouts and add images.
- ❼ Flat-bed process camera adds photos and drawings to page layouts.
- ❽ Photo processing/enlarging/editing controls. Final page layouts are edited here.
- ❾ Camera monitor screen.
- ❿ Photo and drawing insertion trays.
- ⓫ Process camera auto-focusing system.
- ⓬ Paper reel.
- ⓭ Paper reel drum support frame.
- ⓮ Paper reel drum carrying frame: an external crane (not shown) lifts the paper drum into position.
- ⓯ Paper feed controls.
- ⓰ Paper tension and speed control rollers.
- ⓱ Four-colour printing ink containers (cyan, magenta, yellow and black).
- ⓲ Ink distribution valves.
- ⓳ Gravure printing press enclosure.
- ⓴ Ink supply dials.
- 21 Ink regulator controls.
- 22 Ink drying heat chamber.
- 23 Ink drying chamber cooling vent.
- 24 Printing ink heater controls.
- 25 Heat chamber temperature display.
- 26 Paper and ink is cooled here before trimming and binding.
- 27 Paper trimming guillotine (mind fingers!).
- 28 Paper trimming conveyor and guillotine pad.
- 29 Guillotine controls.
- 30 Chop counter.
- 31 Cover binding glue container and automated valve.
- 32 Pre-printed card covers stacked in binding machine.
- 33 Cover binding placement grabs.
- 34 Pages ready for binding.
- 35 Cover binding drum - pages are stacked on the drum's upper angled edge while glue is applied.
- 36 Drum swivels forward after each book is completed and bound, dropping the book down to the packing chute.
- 37 Packing box for finished books, ready for dispatch.

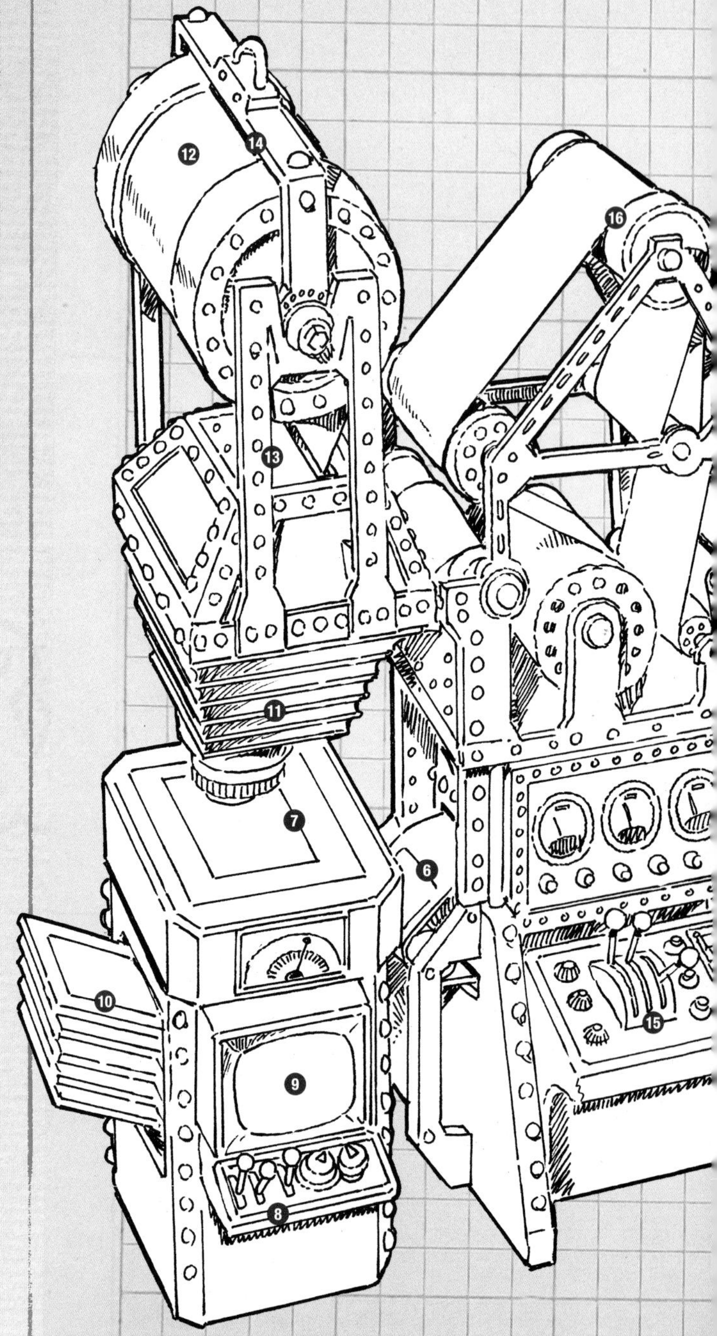
12
14
16
13
11
7
6
10
9
15
8

FOLIO

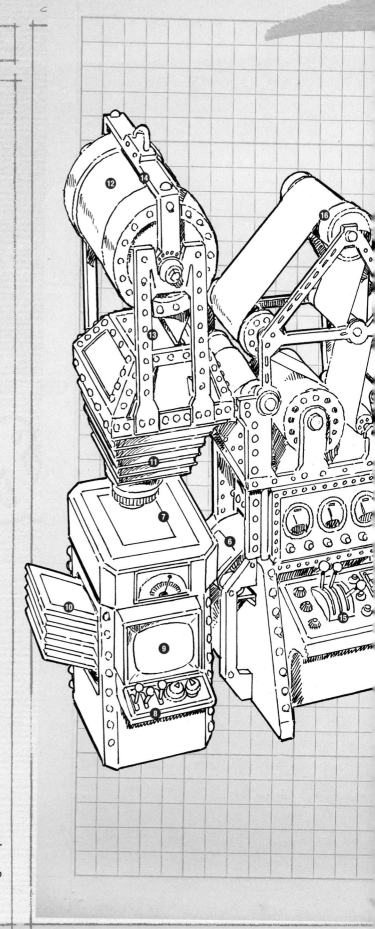

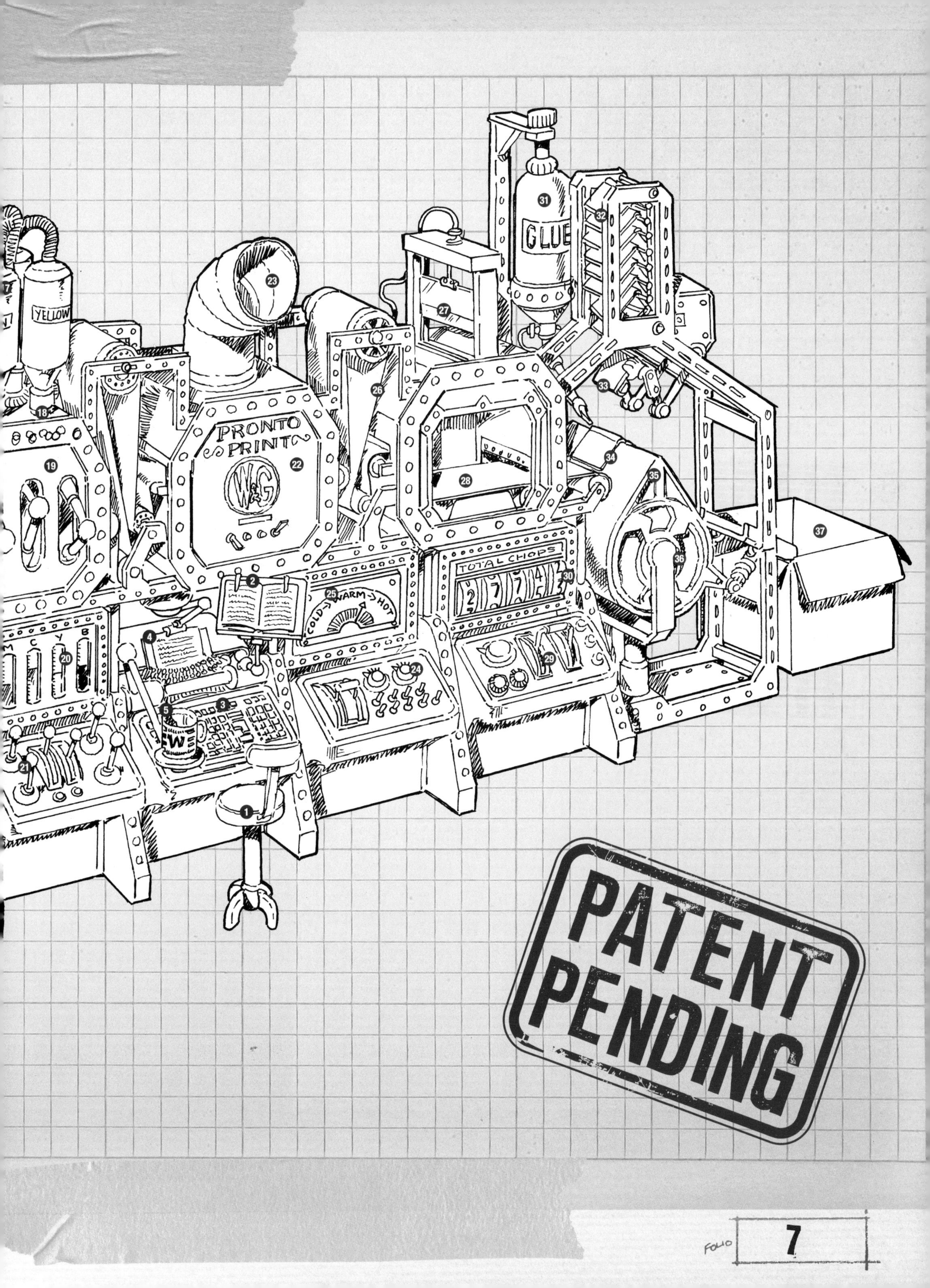
YELLOW
GLUE
PRONTO PRINT
W&G
COLD WARM HOT
TOTAL CHOPS
M C Y B

PATENT PENDING

MAIN HEADING

CELLAR STUDIO

SUB HEADING

Contents

CONTENTS LIST

PAGE NO.

SUB HEADING

General description

BODY COPY

DROP CAP

When Wallace is invited to host a new television programme about inventions, he decides that it would be handy to build the studio in the cellar of 62 West Wallaby Street so that he can demonstrate a few inventions of his own.

The centrepiece is Wallace's presenting workbench, and behind this is the 'World of Invention' main studio set backdrop, which features a rotating globe at its centre surrounded by a contra-rotating series logo. The rotation of these is actuated by a series of large gears behind the backdrop, which are driven by an electric motor.

Studio lighting is suspended from an overhead rig, with additional lights mounted on tripods for ease of positioning. Three studio cameras are employed, which are mounted on dollies in order to follow Wallace around the studio as required. Each programme episode has a 'Curiosity Corner' section, which Wallace presents from an armchair (not shown).

Studio sound and vision mixing is performed by Gromit from a control desk positioned just off camera. Next to this is the programme editing and vision-mixing console, which enables Gromit to cue filmed reports of inventions from around the world. A cooker, grill and kettle are included as part of Gromit's control suite for the supply of tea and cakes during non-live sections of the programme.

On the other side of the studio is a second set backdrop. This conceals the 'Jumbo Generator' (see page 26 for full description), which provides a backup electricity supply in the event of a power cut as well as additional power on demand. Mounted in the centre of this backdrop is a television monitor used for the viewing of outside reports and archive footage. A mechanical hatch covers the screen and opens automatically to reveal it at the start of each film, closing again at the end.

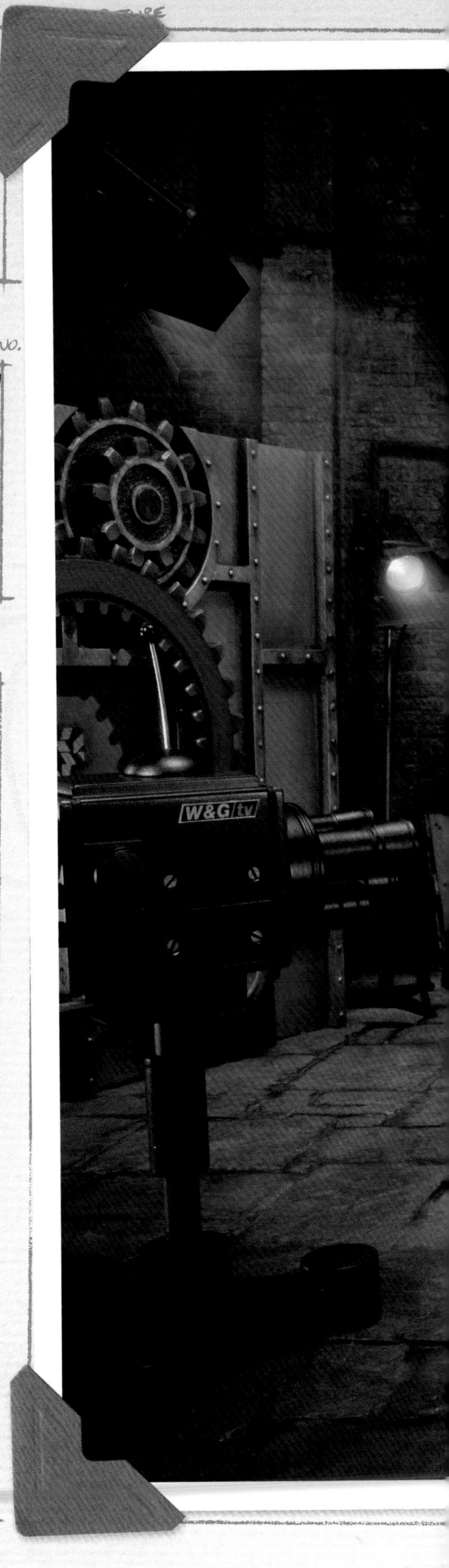

W&G tv

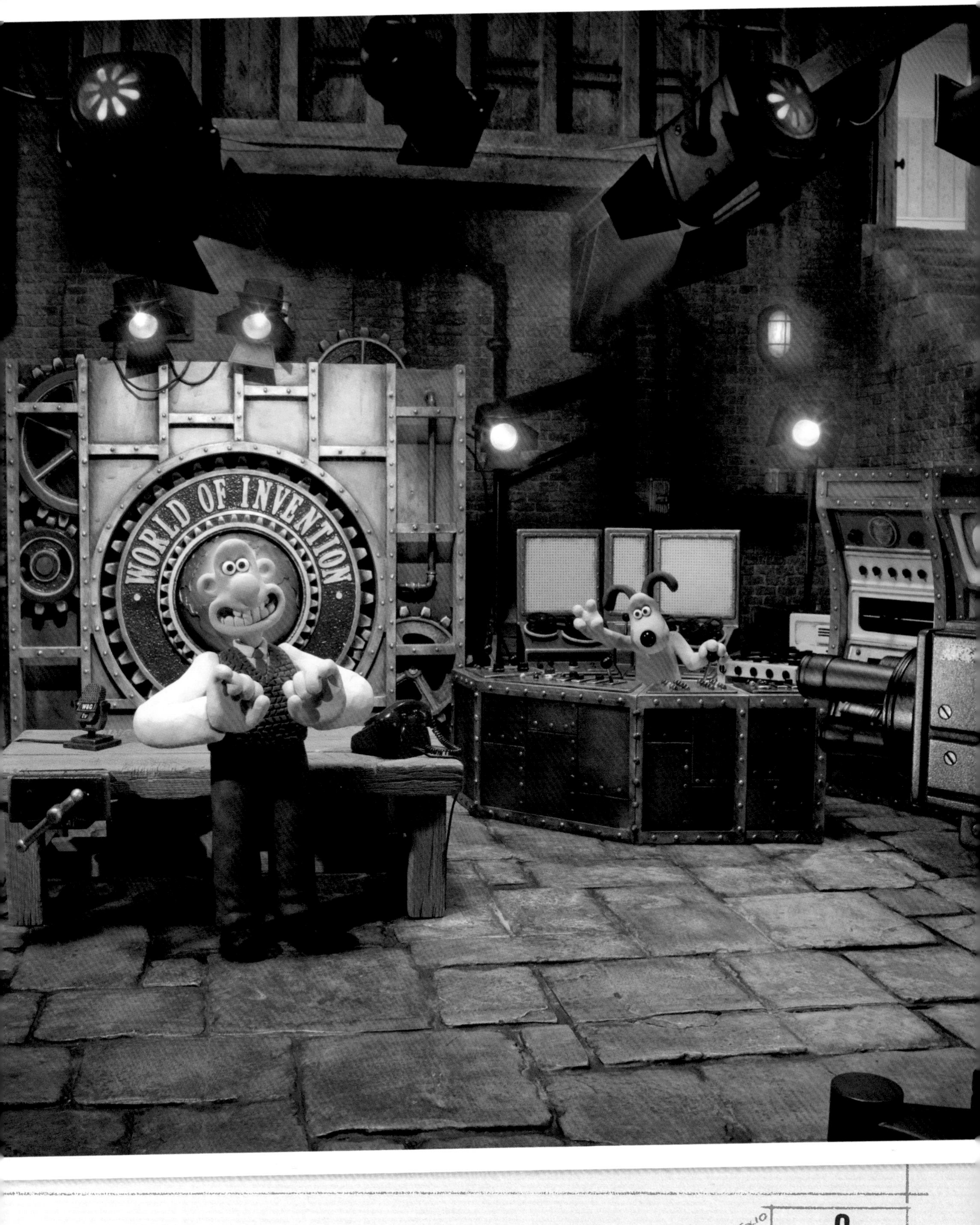
WORLD OF INVENTION

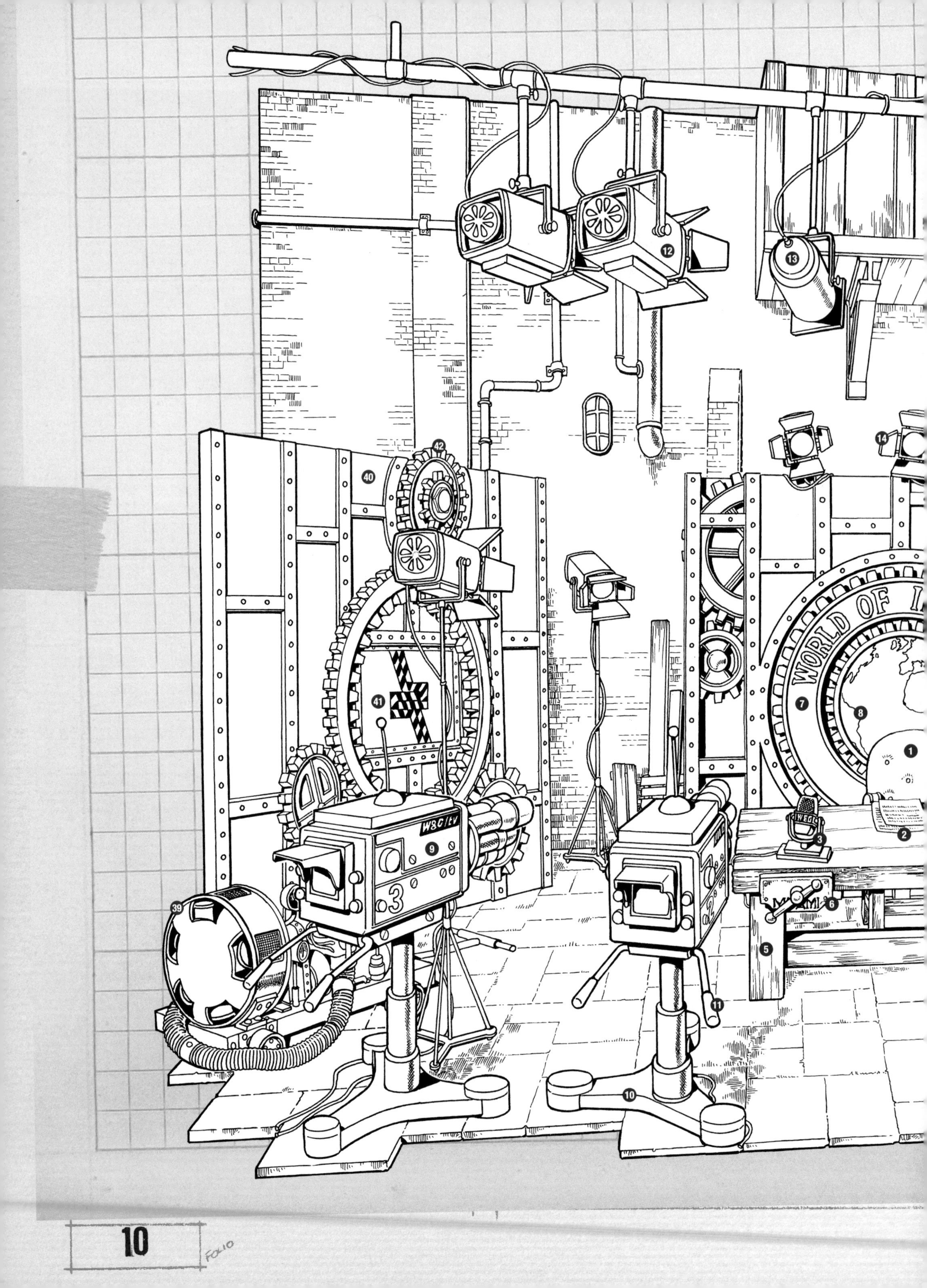
WORLD OF
3
1
2
3
5
6
7
8
9
10
11
12
13
14
39
40
41
42

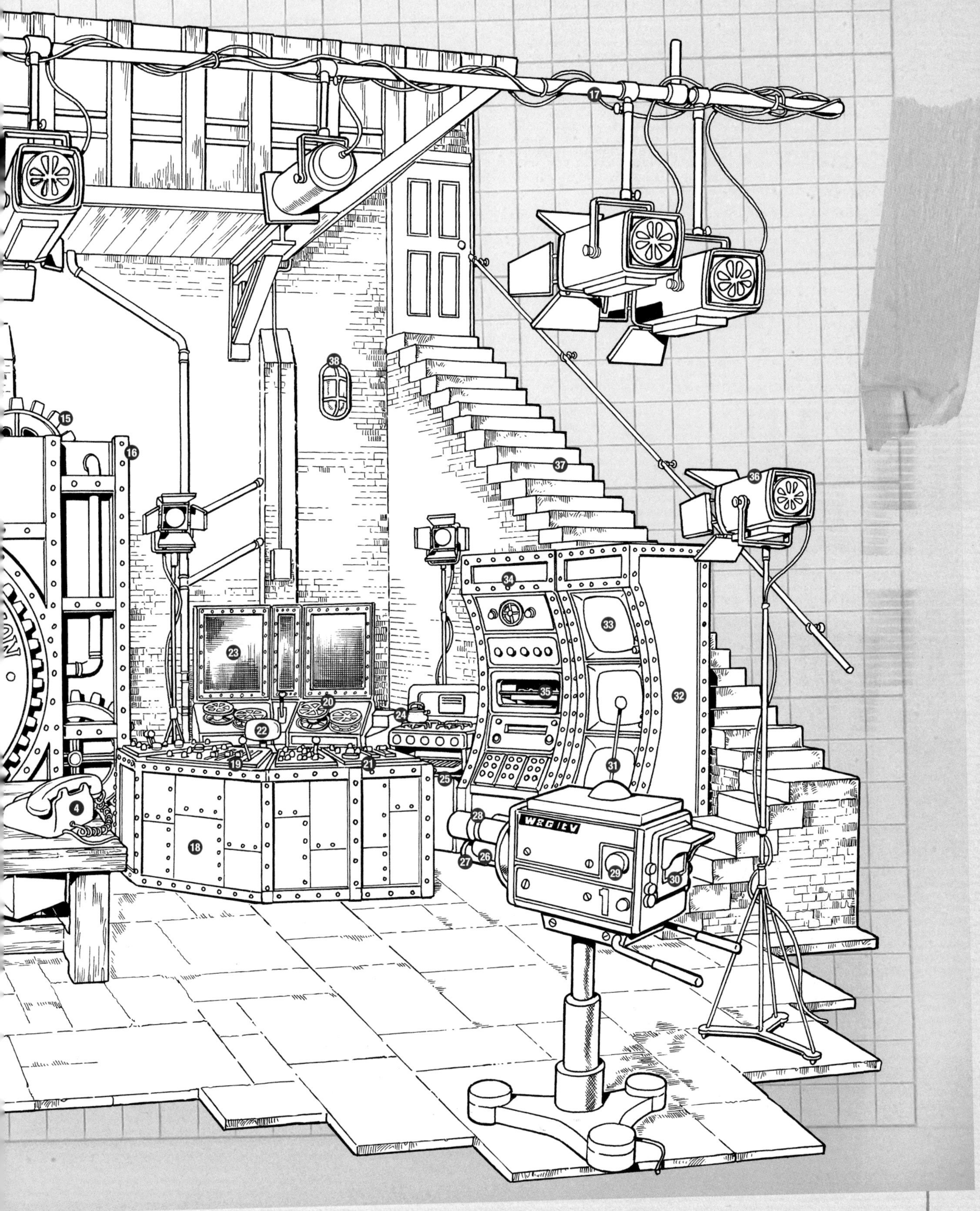
17
38
15
16
37
36
34
33
23
32
35
20
24
22
19
21
31
25
4
28
18
26
27
29
30
1

Cellar Studio

❶ Wallace's presenting chair.

❷ Script.

❸ Microphone.

❹ Telephone linked to outside broadcast units and hotline to programme commissioner.

❺ Wallace's workbench.

❻ Workbench vice, supplied by 'Miami'.

❼ Rotating 'World of Invention' logo.

❽ Revolving globe.

❾ Custom-built W&G TV automatic studio camera Mk-1.

❿ Telescopic and height-adjustable camera dolly.

⓫ Camera movement operating handles.

⓬ Rig-mounted standard studio light.

⓭ Rig-mounted multicolour light.

⓮ Spotlights used for studio backlighting.

⓯ Logo rotation gearing.

⓰ Studio backdrop.

⓱ Lighting rig.

⓲ Studio sound and vision mixing control desk.

⓳ Remote camera controls.

⓴ Sound mixing control console.

㉑ Studio lighting controls.

㉒ Gromit's chair.

㉓ Studio monitor speakers.

㉔ Kettle.

㉕ Cooker for snacks and in-studio cookery demonstrations.

㉖ Long-focus narrow-angle lens.

㉗ Short-focus wide-angle lens.

㉘ Medium/long focus lens.

㉙ Focusing dial.

㉚ Viewfinder.

㉛ Remote control antenna.

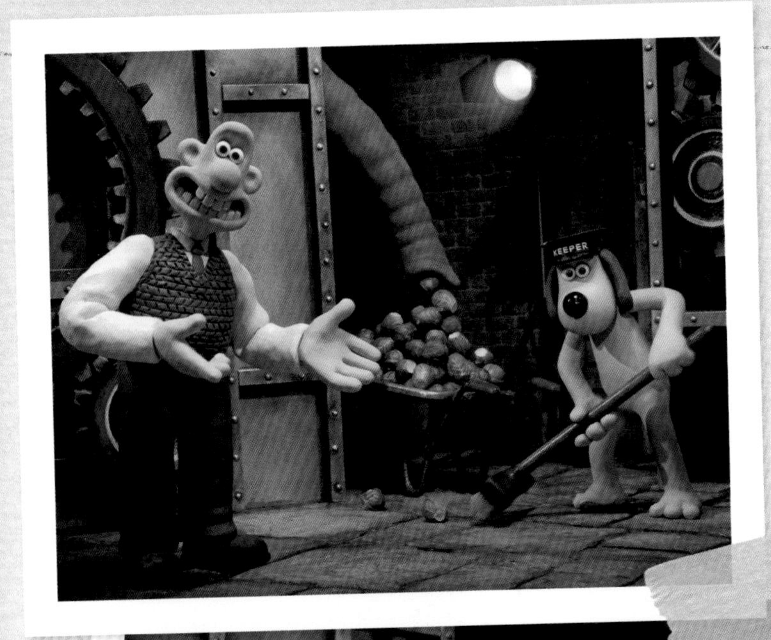
KEEPER

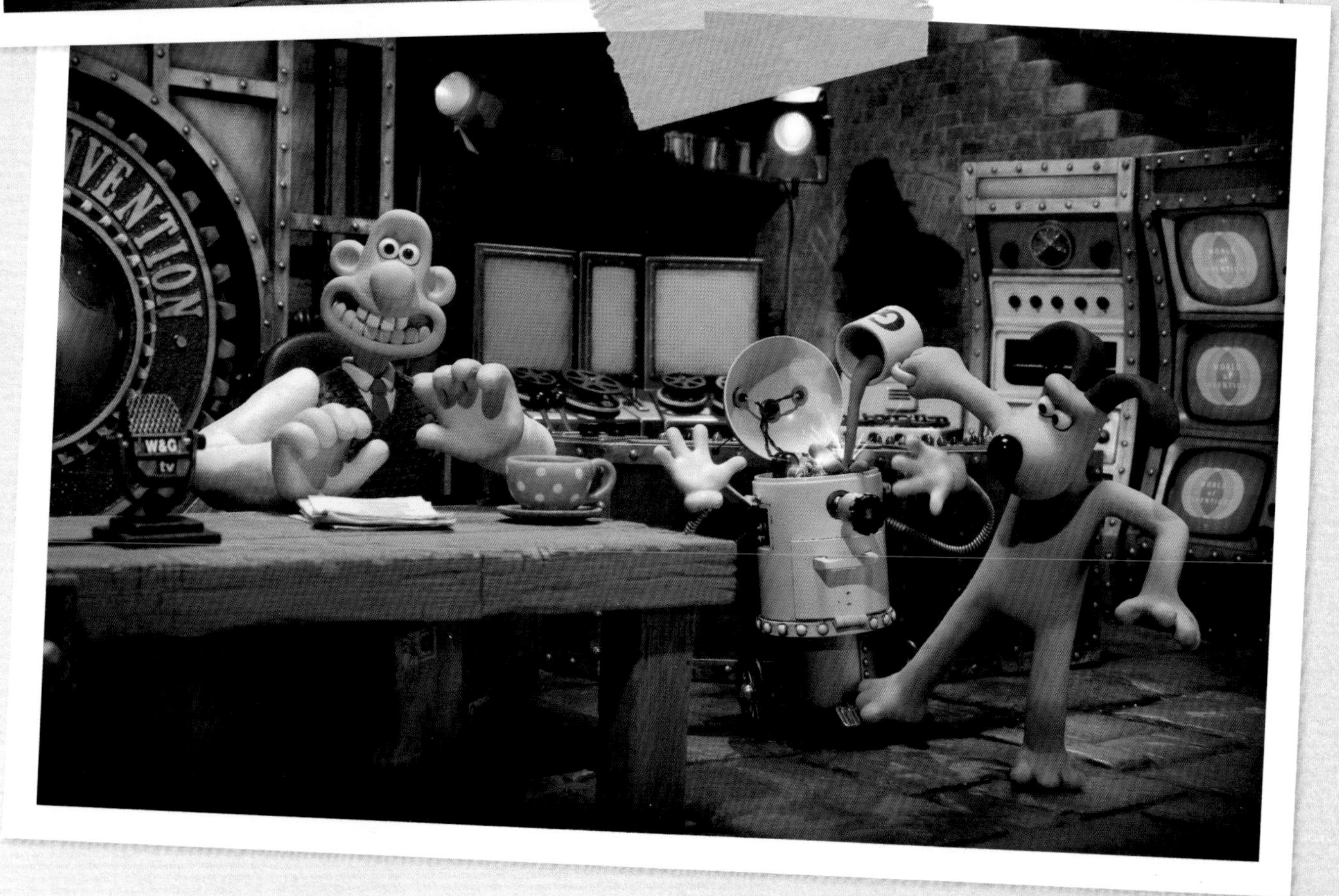
VENTION
W&G
tv

32 Vision mixing console.

33 Monitor screens show output from studio cameras.

34 Programme editing console.

35 Grill.

36 Tripod-mounted studio light.

37 Stairs to ground floor of house.

38 Standard cellar light.

39 Methane-powered 'Jumbo Generator'.

40 Secondary studio set backdrop.

41 Television monitor installed behind sliding hatch.

42 Gearing for monitor hatch mechanism.

ROCKET Mk-2

Contents

General description

The moon rocket is one of Wallace's most ambitious inventions, and it remains one of his finest. So it is no surprise that he keeps it "spaceship shape and Bristol fashion". In fact, not only has the rocket been carefully looked after over the years but it has also undergone a substantial refit since its first lunar excursion.

The modifications have addressed several weaknesses in the original design, and include changes to the engine room and the additions of an auto-locking lower deck access hatch and a staircase linking the upper and lower decks. While the basic structure and outer hull of the rocket remain largely unchanged, slight modifications have been made to the three stabilising fins to improve flight control and comfort upon leaving and re-entering the Earth's atmosphere.

Communications systems have been significantly overhauled, and the original transistor radio has been replaced by an integrated audio-visual communications console, in order to maintain contact with 'mission control' at 62 West Wallaby Street. Flight and navigation controls are carried over from the previous model although a new state-of-the-art cheese detection device enables more accurate targeting of appropriate lunar landing sites.

For the crew, several important improvements have been made to the cabin on the upper deck, and particularly in respect of home comforts. Extra storage for tea, cheese and crackers was considered a priority, along with a larger (tea-making) water tank for extended journeys. Finally, cabin lighting has been upgraded from a single standard lamp to fixed wall lights with tasteful shades.

Although the rocket can be launched and controlled completely from the cabin as before, a remote-control system has been added. This allows the rocket and any occupants (willing or otherwise) to be launched into space at the push of a desk-mounted button.

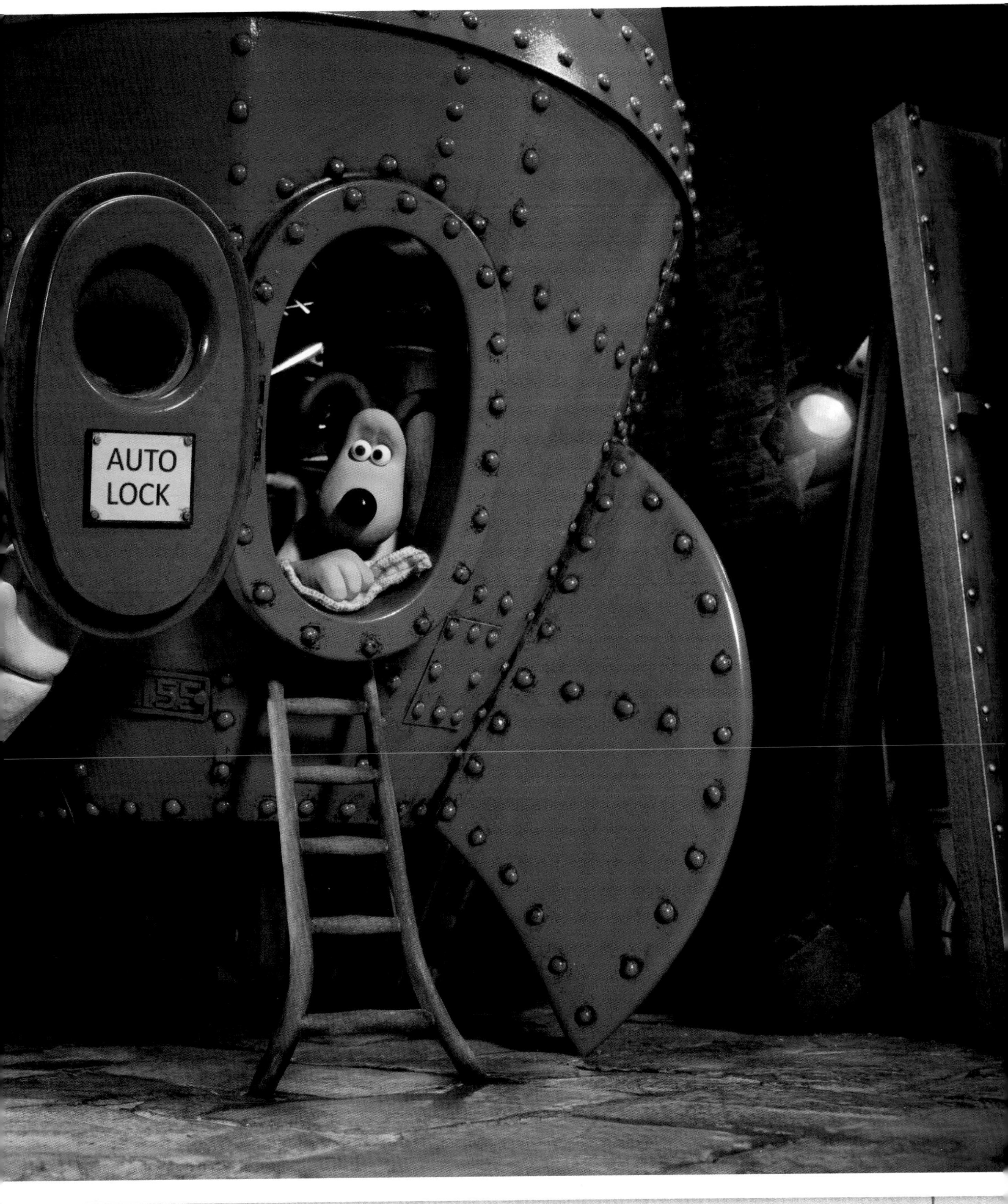
AUTO
LOCK

Rocket Mk-2

BULLET LIST

❶ Stabilising fin (one of three) now incorporates aerodynamic points for extra stability in flight.

❷ Lower deck access ladder in stowed position.

❸ Folding step ladder on lower deck, used for access to upper deck from ground level.

❹ Pressurised lower deck access hatch.

❺ Rocket engine.

❻ Engine manual controls.

❼ Water tank.

❽ Cabin air tanks.

❾ Access staircase between upper and lower decks.

❿ Access hatch between upper and lower decks.

⓫ Observation porthole.

⓬ Acceleration/relaxation chair.

⓭ Cabin lighting.

⓮ Upper deck exit hatch.

⓯ Hull support stanchion.

⓰ Radio telephone communications console.

⓱ Video communications controls.

⓲ Video communications camera.

⓳ Video and audio connecting cables.

⓴ Video communications CRT monitor.

㉑ Video and radio communications antenna (compact indoor type).

㉒ Kettle and teapot.

㉓ Cheese dish and cheese supply.

㉔ Cheese crackers supply.

㉕ Wallace's tea mug.

㉖ Cheese detection device antenna.

㉗ Cheese detection device, used to verify types of cheese on lunar excursions.

㉘ Flight control console systems monitor screen.

㉙ Control systems console seat.

㉚ Rocket control systems console.

㉛ Gromit's tea mug.

㉜ Control system mechanics.

㉝ Tea supplies storage.

㉞ Engine room light switch.

㉟ First-aid box.

㊱ Fuel feed pipe.

㊲ Fuel tank.

㊳ Fuel distribution/regulation valve.

㊴ Fly by wire/elastic band control systems.

FO

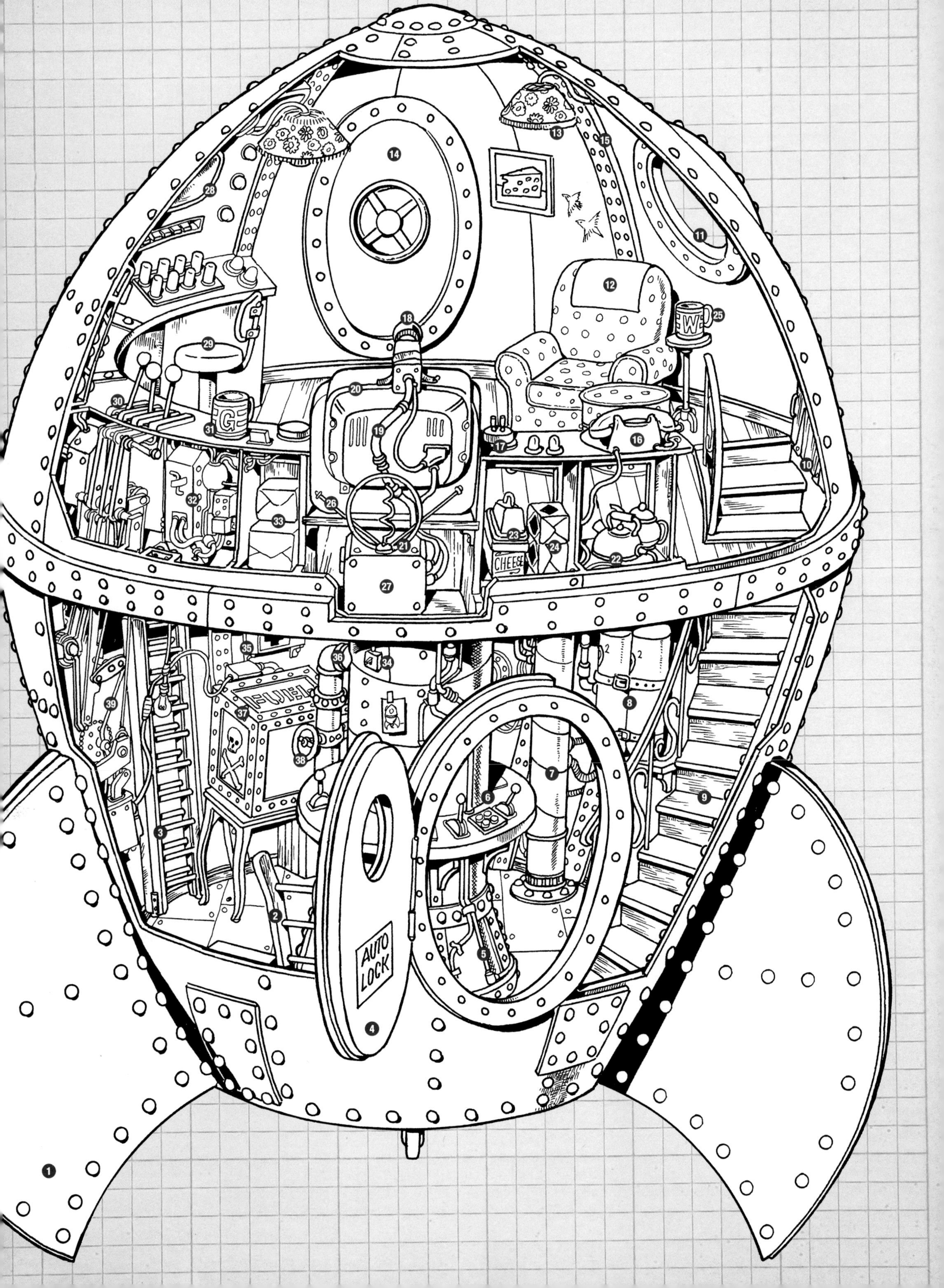
FUEL
CHEESE
AUTO LOCK

MAIN HEADING

L.A.D.

SUB HEADING

Contents

CONTENTS LIST PAGE NO

SUB HEADING

General description

DROP CAP BODY COPY

Many inventors imagine a future where robots carry out all the household chores while we enjoy a life of leisure. Wallace's contribution to this dream is the Labour Assisting Device or L.A.D., which was built to perform various duties around the studio during the filming of the 'World of Invention' television series.

L.A.D.'s basic construction comprises a short, cylindrical body with a domed top. It is able to move around freely using two large drive wheels, one on each side, with a smaller, rear-mounted wheel for balance. Each drive wheel is mounted on a half axle and driven from the main motor via speed control gearing. This enables L.A.D. to move forwards and backwards, and make turns of any radius, even turning on the spot if required.

Three hatches (one each side plus one at the front) open to allow the deployment of five separate articulated arms. Two arms are deployed from each side hatch and one from the front hatch. Each arm is carried and stowed on a deployment reel, and can be extended fully or partially as necessary. At the end of each arm is a gloved hand featuring four articulated fingers for grasping.

Protruding from the front of L.A.D.'s upper casing is an articulated and telescopic visual processing camera lens. This captures all visual information and supplies it to the primary functions circuit boards (the 'brain'), which are linked directly to the memory bank and processing circuits.

All mechanical functions are driven by a single motor, and a complex arrangement of gears and clutches supply drive to individual components, such as the drive wheels and the arm deployment reels.

L.A.D. operates independently for the most part but can be programmed to perform specific tasks using a hand-held remote control. Maintenance is carried out via any of the three arm hatches, or by opening the entire domed top section using a foot-operated pedal at the front of the device. However, care must be exercised when working on the sensitive circuits in the domed top section, which are susceptible to damage by moisture in particular.

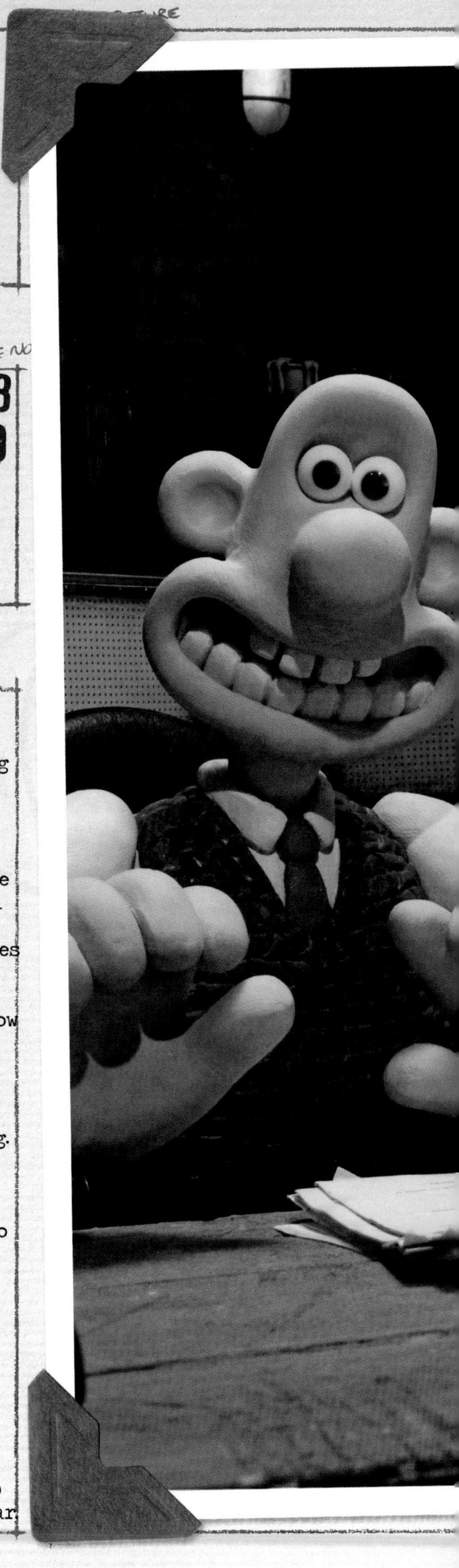

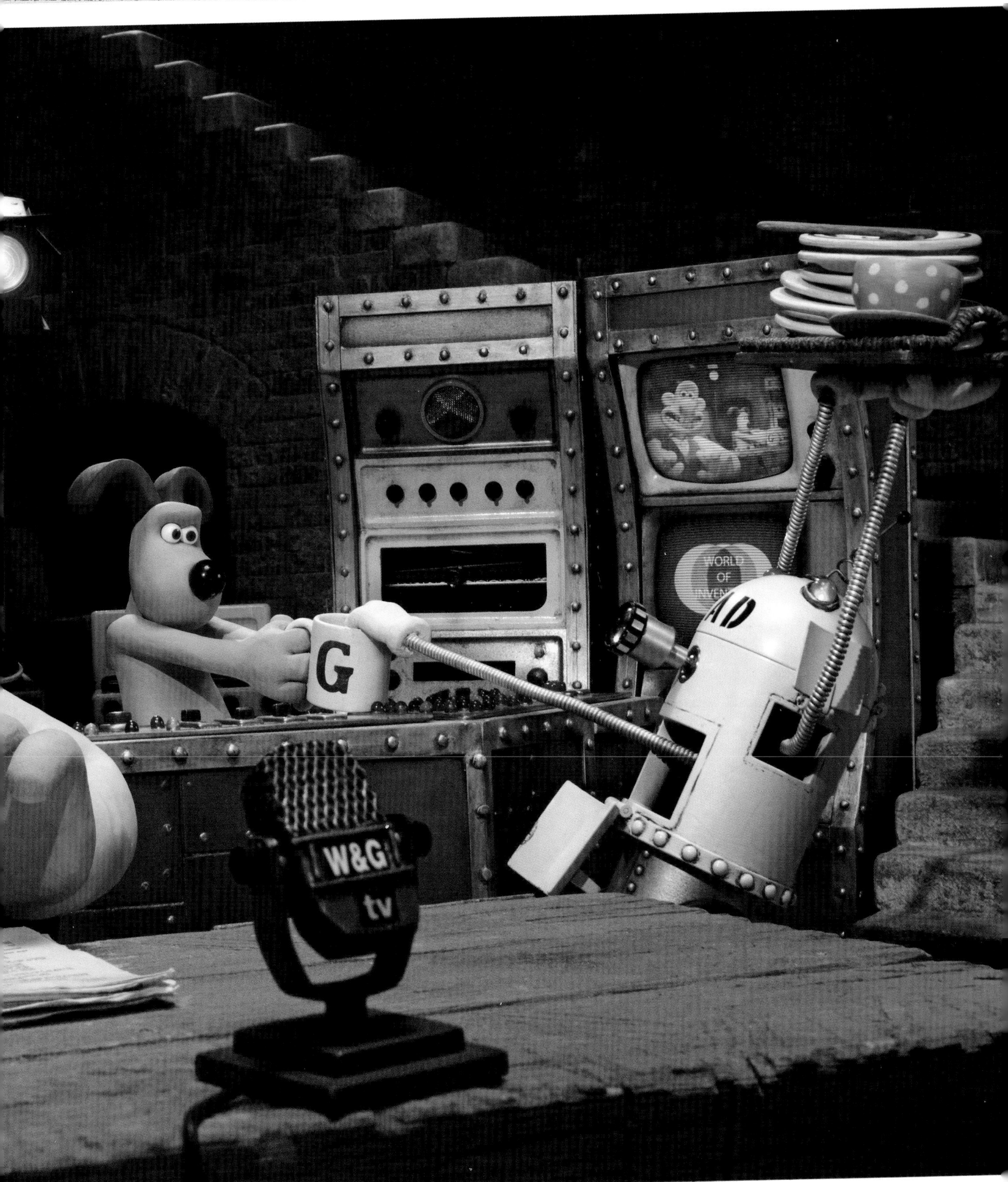
G
W&G
tv

L.A.D.

BULLET LIST

❶ Antenna linking Wallace's remote to the L.A.D. Primary functions.

❷ Memory bank and program processing circuits.

❸ Indicator light power cables.

❹ Power indicator lights.

❺ Transformer coils.

❻ Fully articulated visual processing auto-focus camera lens.

❼ Visual processing conduits.

❽ L.A.D. Primary functions circuit boards controlling arm movement and speed/direction functions (linked to remote via antenna).

❾ Left arm hatch.

❿ Lower left arm deployed.

⓫ Hands fitted with white butler gloves for clean service.

⓬ Upper left arm in stowed position inside deployment reel.

⓭ Arm reel deployment gearing.

⓮ Right arm hatch also provides maintenance access to L.A.D.'s upper section.

⓯ Deployed upper right arm.

⓰ Arm movement control wiring.

⓱ Lower right arm in stowed position.

⓲ Left side battery.

⓳ Right side battery.

⓴ Forward arm deployment reel.

㉑ Forward arm deployment reel rotation gearing.

㉒ Finger manipulation and control actuators.

㉓ Foot-operated upper dome hatch pedal.

㉔ Dome hatch pedal linkage.

㉕ Upper dome section hinge: dome opens to allow access to L.A.D. control circuitry.

㉖ Forward hatch in lowered position allows forward arm deployment and maintenance access.

㉗ Electric motor drives all mechanical functions.

㉘ Speed control gearing.

㉙ Rear-mounted balancing wheel.

L.A.D. Remote Control

❶ L.A.D. rotary function selector and programming dial.

❷ Emergency programming override switch.

❸ Upper and lower right manipulation arm control on/off switches.

❹ Upper and lower left manipulation arm control on/off switches.

❺ L.A.D. main power switch.

❻ Telescopic remote control command antenna.

❼ Antenna safety tip.

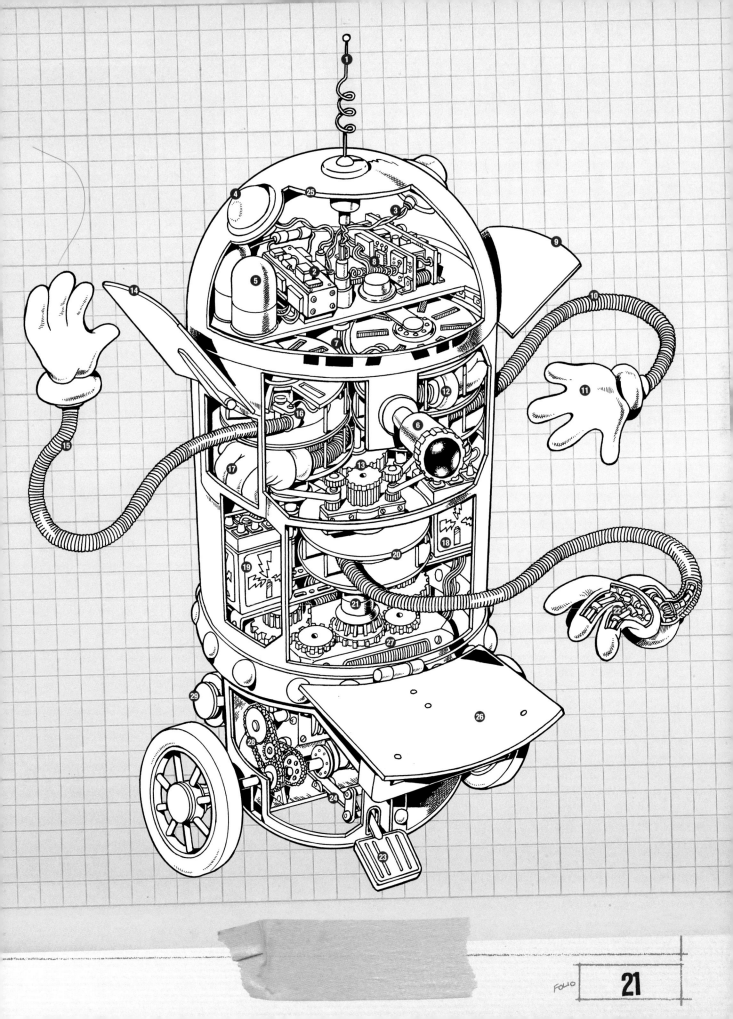

MAIN HEADING

RUNABOUT STEAM CHAIR

SUB HEADING

Contents

CONTENTS LIST

PAGE NO.

SUB HEADING

General description

BODY COPY

DROP CAP

The Runabout Steam Chair is Wallace's prototype for personal motorised transport. It is compact, manoeuvrable and easy to operate although reliability can be an issue. Because it is designed to carry one person, who controls all functions from a seat at the front of the machine, an assistant is also required to act as fireman, keeping the fire stoked and fuelled with coal.

The general principle of operation can be compared to any conventional steam engine. Water is turned into superheated steam by the boiler and fed via pipes to the piston cylinders, which are mounted either side of the vehicle. The amount of steam entering each cylinder is independently controlled by the operator using two regulator handles at the front of the vehicle. The steam enters each cylinder through a reciprocating valve assembly, forcing the piston and connecting rod to move, which in turn causes the front wheel to rotate. On its return stroke, the piston forces the steam back out of the cylinder, through the valve, and up the exhaust blast pipe. The cycle is then repeated until the supply of steam is cut off.

When both regulator handles are moved to the same position, the same amount of steam is allowed into each cylinder causing both front wheels to move by the same amount. Hence, the vehicle is propelled forward in a straight line. Turns are effected by reducing the amount of steam entering one cylinder, thereby slowing the rotation of the wheel on that side. The resulting speed differential between the wheels causes the vehicle to turn. A hand-operated brake lever is fitted to each regulator handle, which provides instantaneous steam cut-off for sudden stops. The rear end of the vehicle is supported by a single pivoted castor wheel, which allows very tight turning circles.

The operator's seat is padded and heat-resistant for comfort, and it can be raised on a vertically mounted steam piston to provide access to high shelves around the home or workshop.

FOLIO

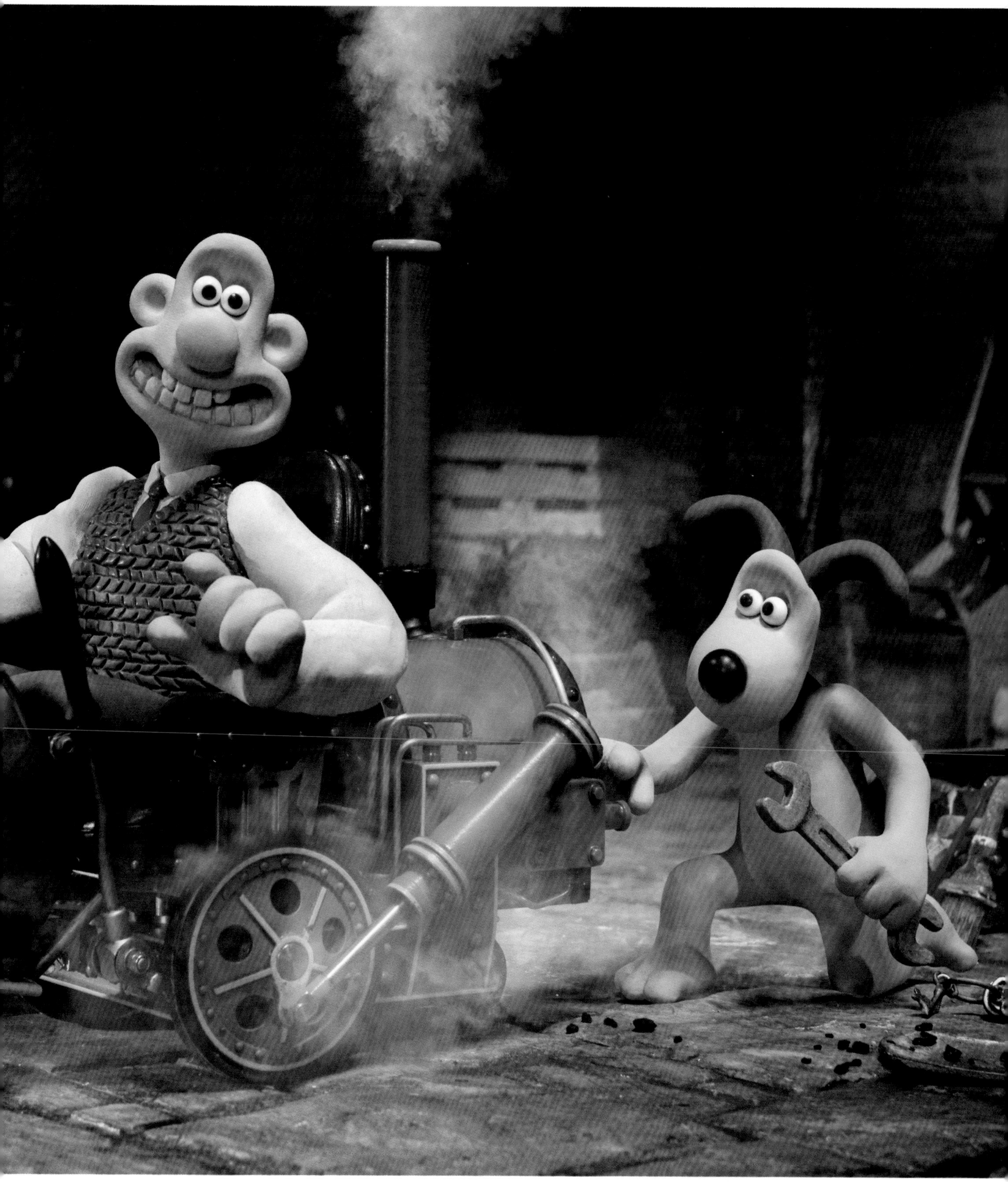

SUB HEADING

Runabout Steam Chair

BULLET LIST

1. Steam dome.
2. Superheater tubes.
3. Steam pipes to cylinders.
4. Superheater header.
5. Exhaust blast pipe from cylinders.
6. Chimney cowl.
7. Rear-mounted valve tap provides boiling water for essentials like tea.
8. Firebox (also good for fry-up).
9. Piston valve housing.
10. Piston cylinder.

CUTAWAY HERE

11. Water tank.
12. Connecting rod to drive wheels.
13. Large front-mounted fixed wheels provide forward and reverse drive as well as steering.
14. Rear-mounted pivoted castor wheel.
15. Steam chair operator's padded, heat-resistant seat.
16. Padded, heat-resistant backrest.
17. Support frame.
18. Armrests for elbow support.
19. Independent steam regulator handles.
20. Braking handles.
21. Footplate.

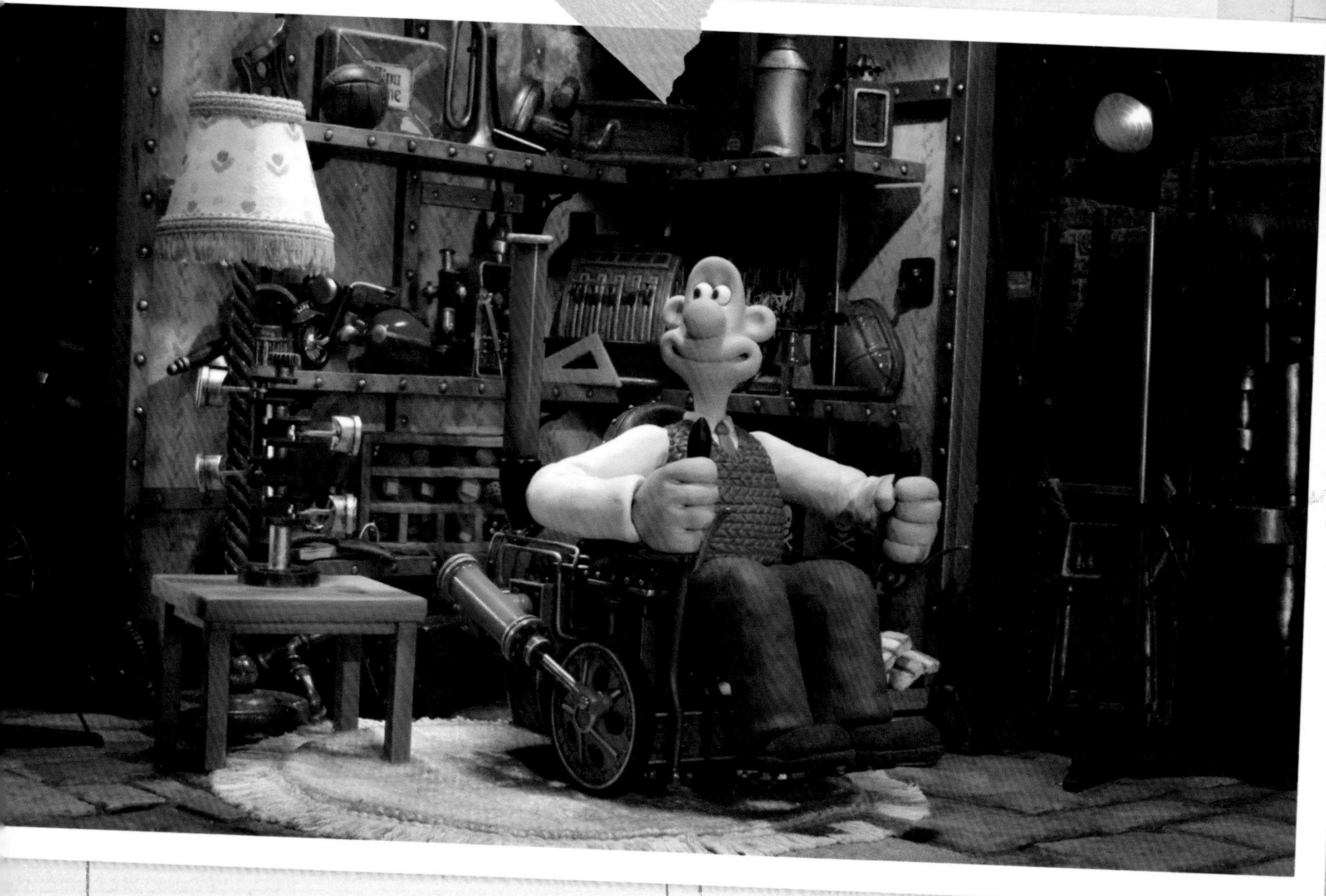

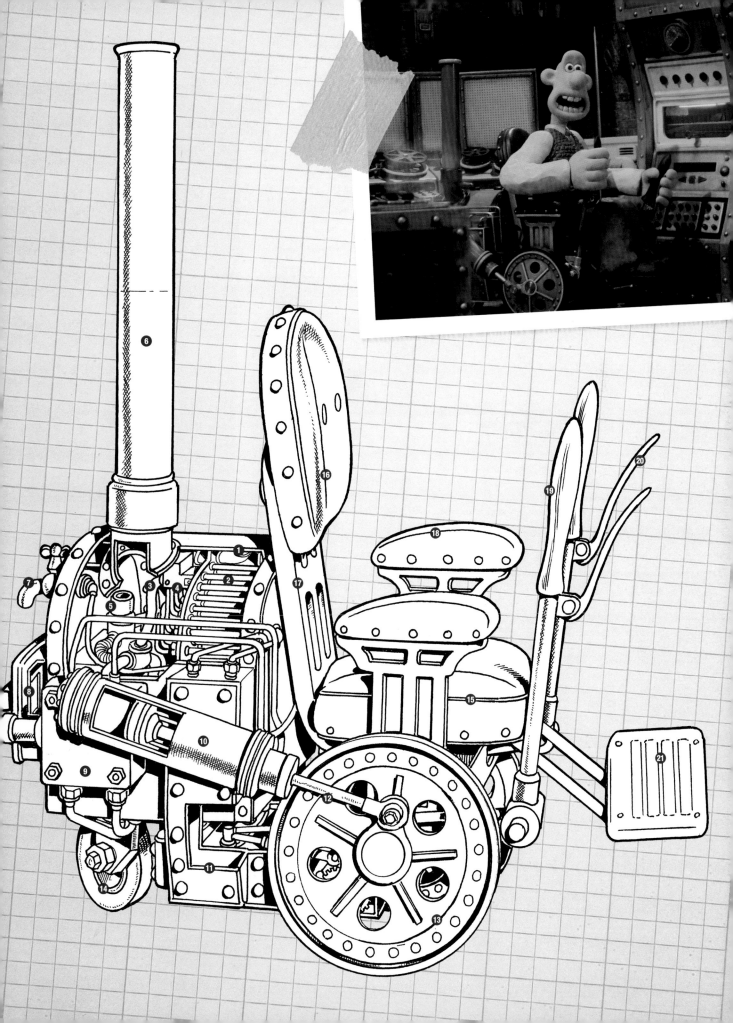

MAIN HEADING

JUMBO GENERATOR

MINIATURE

SUB HEADING

General description

BODY COPY

DROP CAP

It is well documented how mammals can turn leafy vegetables into methane gas. Perhaps less well known is that the process is particularly efficient in the case of elephants. With the Jumbo Generator, Wallace created a remarkable, if somewhat unorthodox, solution to the huge power demands of the television studio in his cellar.

The structure of the machine consists of a large riveted steel frame, which is designed to hold the elephant (Kevin) in position via a spring-mounted adjustable neck collar. It is essential that this collar is fitted correctly, with enough slack to allow two adult arms to be inserted between it and the elephant's neck. At the rear end is a similarly sprung collection dome, which is shaped for maximum comfort and flexibility. A reinforced wooden platform provides a sturdy base for Kevin to stand on as well as protection for the studio cabling that runs beneath it. The front of the frame is covered to shield Kevin from view and forms part of Wallace's studio set. In the centre of the front wall a television monitor is mounted behind a twin-sliding-door hatch, which opens and closes as required.

Brussels sprouts are used as the 'input' fuel due to their convenience and high yield. The methane gas is collected in the collection dome and fed via a flexible hose to the generator. A pressure valve is fitted to regulate the supply of methane to the generator, which is driven by a reciprocating two-cylinder, air-cooled engine. A cranking handle is provided to start the engine by hand, after which it runs until the supply of methane is cut off. Electric power is created by the generator and fed via cables to the studio's main power distribution board. The entire engine/generator assembly is mounted on a trolley for ease of positioning.

Provided with a willing elephant and a ready supply of sprouts from the allotment, this simple yet effective device is able to cope with all of Wallace's energy needs.

FOLIO

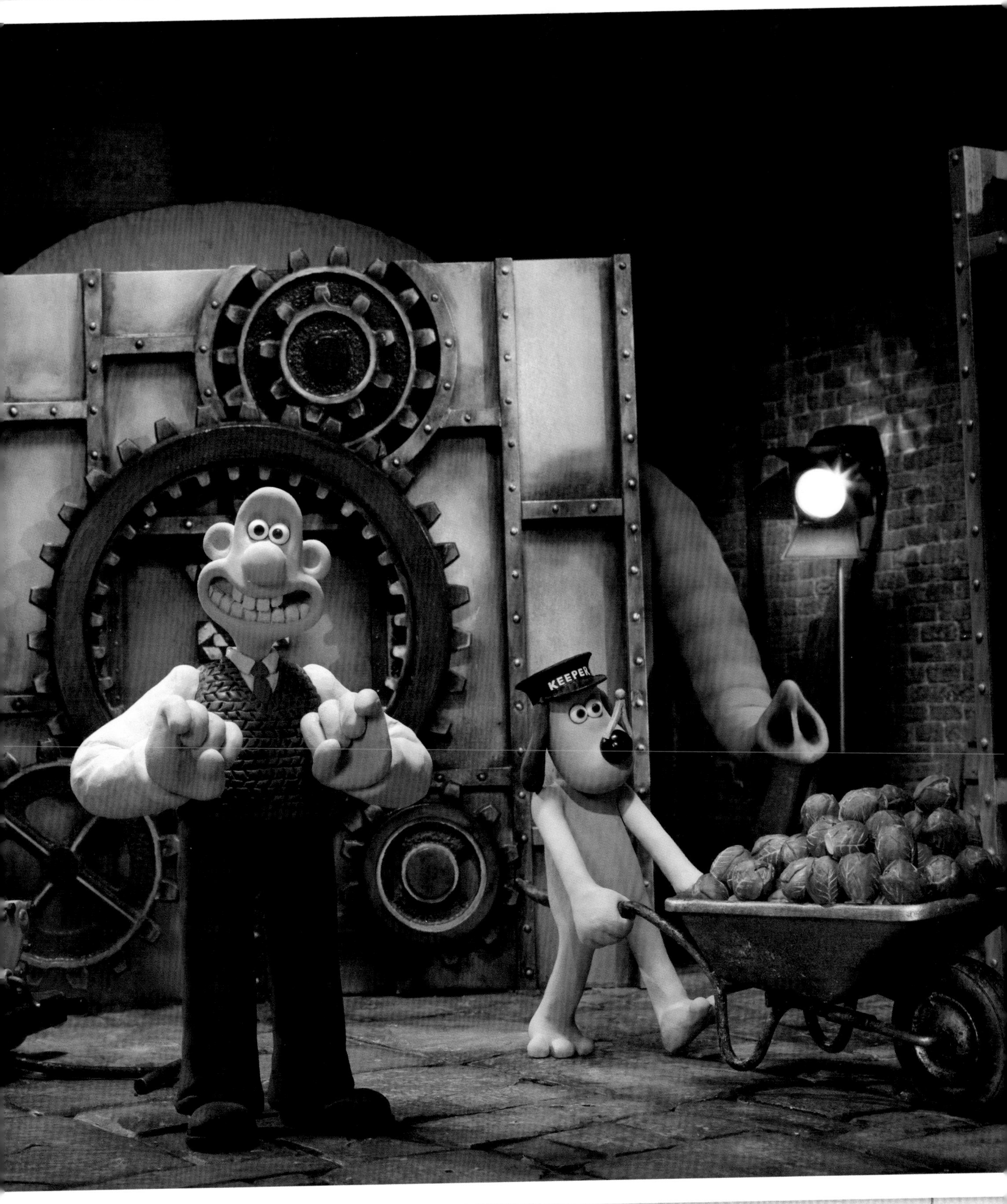
KEEPER

Jumbo Generator

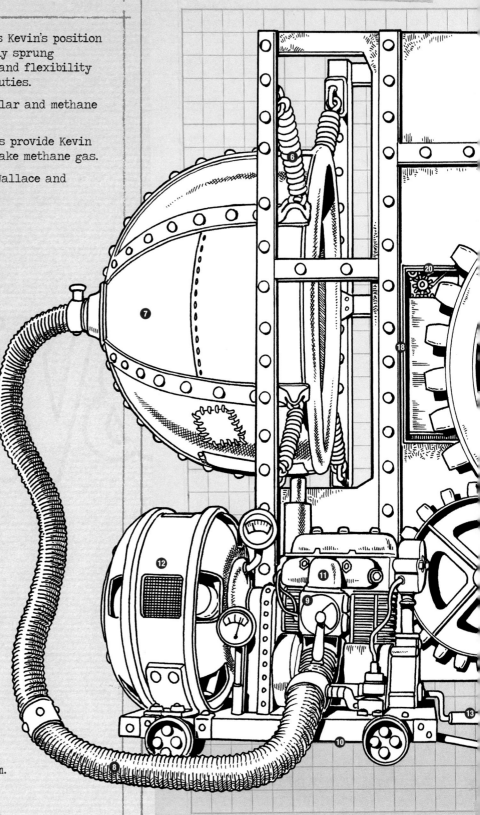

1. Adjustable collar maintain's Kevin's position on the Jumbo Generator. Fully sprung connectors provide comfort and flexibility during Kevin's generating duties.

2. Rear frame supports the collar and methane gas collection dome.

3. Sprouts and other vegetables provide Kevin with the raw materials to make methane gas.

4. Wheelbarrow borrowed from Wallace and Gromit's allotment.

5. Reinforced platform.

6. Sprung collection dome connectors.

7. Methane gas collection dome.

8. Flexible methane gas collection hose.

9. Methane gas pressure valve.

10. Generator trolley.

11. Generator engine.

12. Generator (driven by engine).

13. Starting handle.

14. Underfloor cabling leading to studio's power supply.

15. Cog system powered by generator allows the television monitor hatch doors to slide open while providing visual interest to Wallace's viewers.

16. Television monitor.

17. Televsion monitor connection cables.

18. TV monitor hatch door slot (used when doors are open).

19. TV monitor hatch in closed position.

20. Hatch sliding cog mechanism.

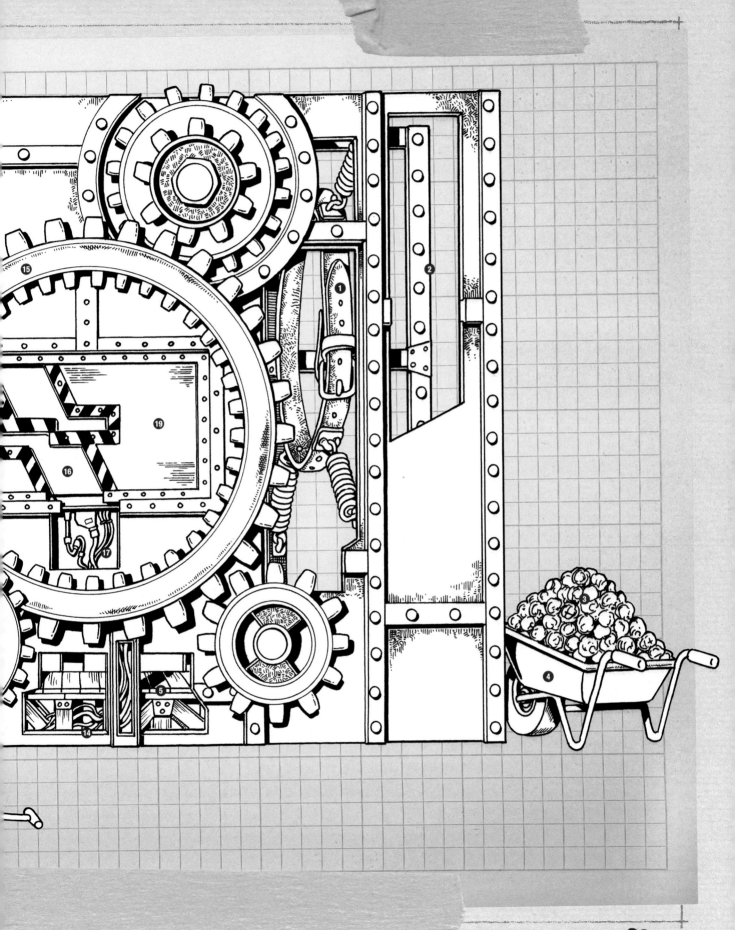

MAIN HEADING

INFLATABLE SAFETY SUIT

SUB HEADING

Contents

CONTENTS LIST

PAGE NO.

SUB HEADING

General description

BODY COPY

DROP CAP

The "total protection hazard-free safety suit" represents a new leap forward in personal accident avoidance. Following a single, sharp tug on the activation cord, the wearer is rendered "instantly impervious to harm".

The suit itself is constructed in one piece from gusseted elasticated fabric, which is based on underwear technology. All joins are supported by carefully designed 'anti-chafe' flexible rubber ribs, which serve to maintain the shape of the suit and provide additional strength and protection upon deployment.

Activation is by means of the aforementioned activation cord, and this is easily located thanks to its bright red triangular hand grip. Pulling the cord activates the igniter. This causes separately stored compounds of sodium azide and potassium nitrate to combine (IMPORTANT: SEE BELOW). The resulting chemical reaction releases a vast amount of nitrogen gas, which inflates the safety suit, encompassing the wearer in an all-round 'air cushion'. Total deployment time is practically instantaneous at around one tenth of a second or less, after which the wearer is fully protected by the inflated suit.

The suit remains inflated indefinitely. Leakage at the neck, wrists and ankles is prevented by tight-fitting anti-deflation gussets, which stretch as the suit expands. For maximum operator comfort, both before and after activation, the wearing of only a string vest under the suit is recommended.

On the whole, the safety suit is simple, ingenious and almost completely successful. The one weakness is the hazard posed to it (and the wearer) by sharp objects, with discarded drawing pins proving to be particularly troublesome, as Wallace discovers when demonstrating the suit during an episode of his 'World of Invention' television show.

(IMPORTANT SAFETY NOTE: DO NOT TRY THIS AT HOME! On no account should readers attempt to recreate the igniter reaction employed by the safety suit.)

MAIN PICTURE

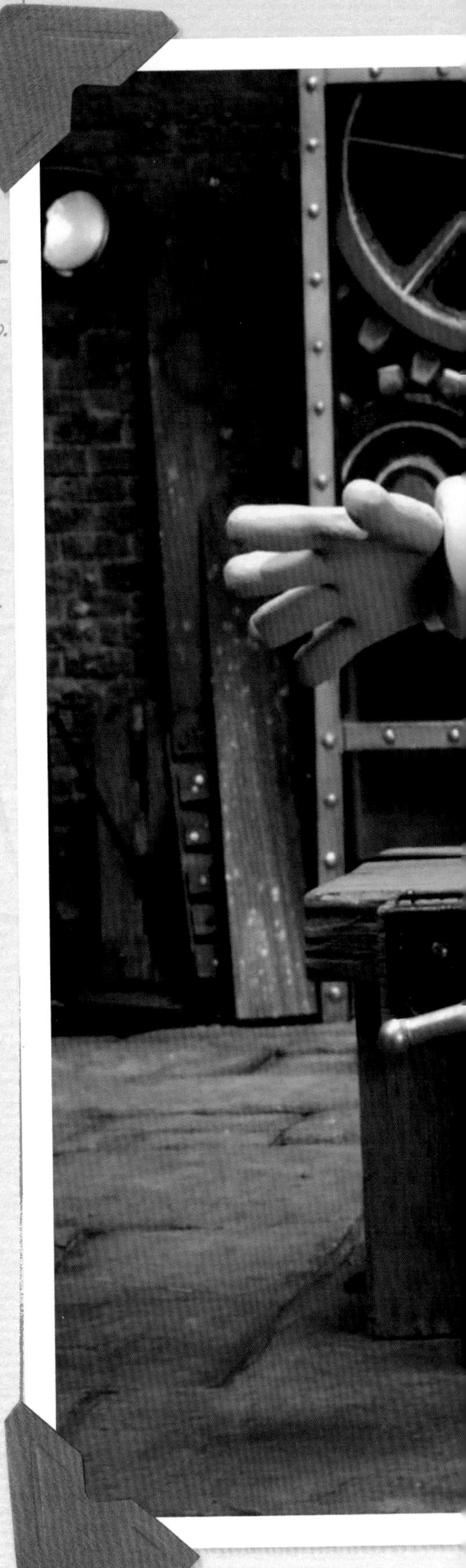

FOLIO

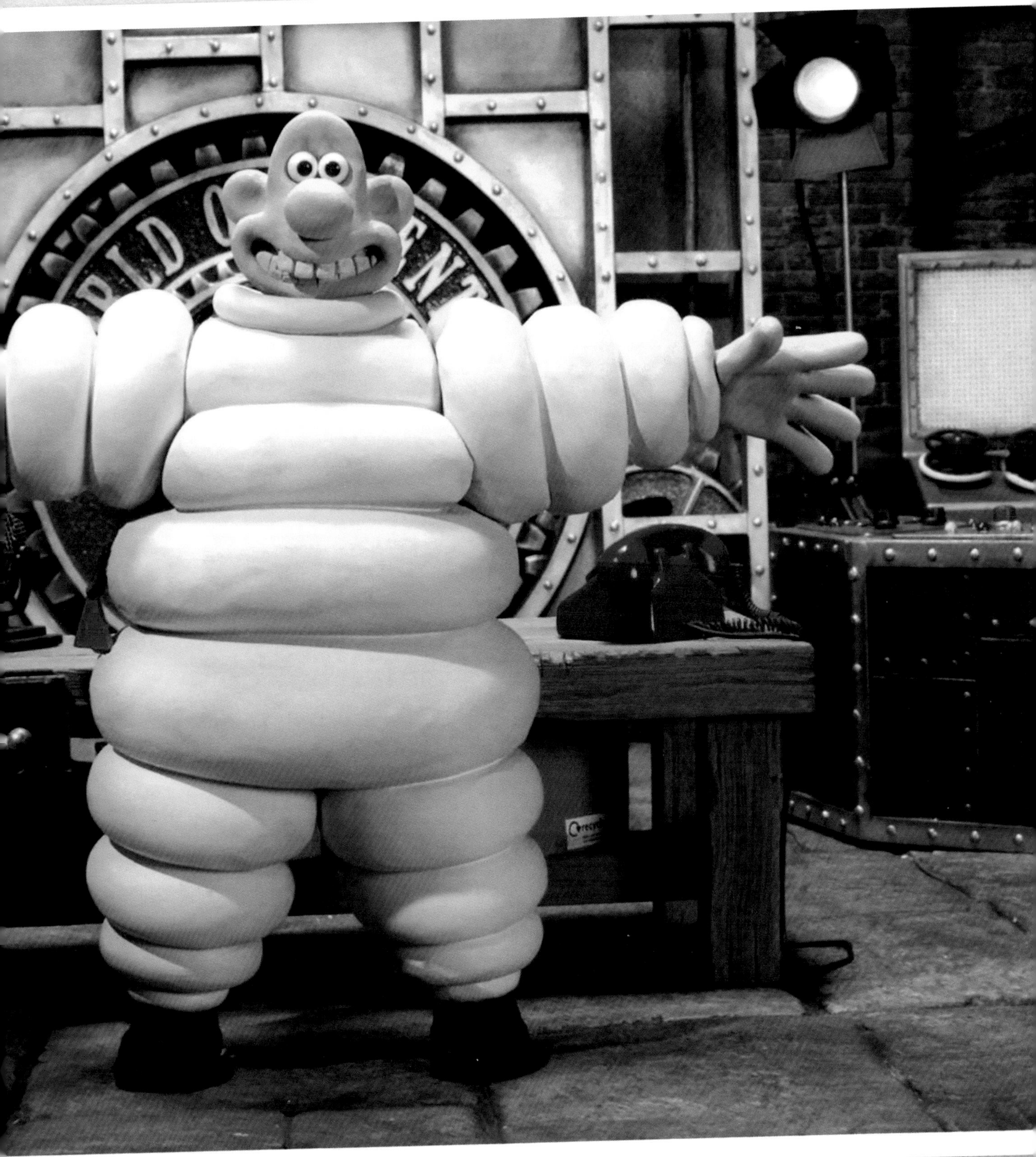

SUB HEADING

CUTAWAY HERE

Inflatable Safety Suit

BULLET LIST

1. Activation cord.
2. Igniter.
3. Sodium azide compound.
4. Potassium nitrate compound.
5. Anti-deflation flexible rubber neck gusset.
6. Anti-deflation wrist gusset.
7. Anti-deflation ankle gusset.
8. Anti-chafe flexible rubber suit ribbing.
9. Easy-inflate balloon fabric based on underwear technology.
10. Wallace's boots.

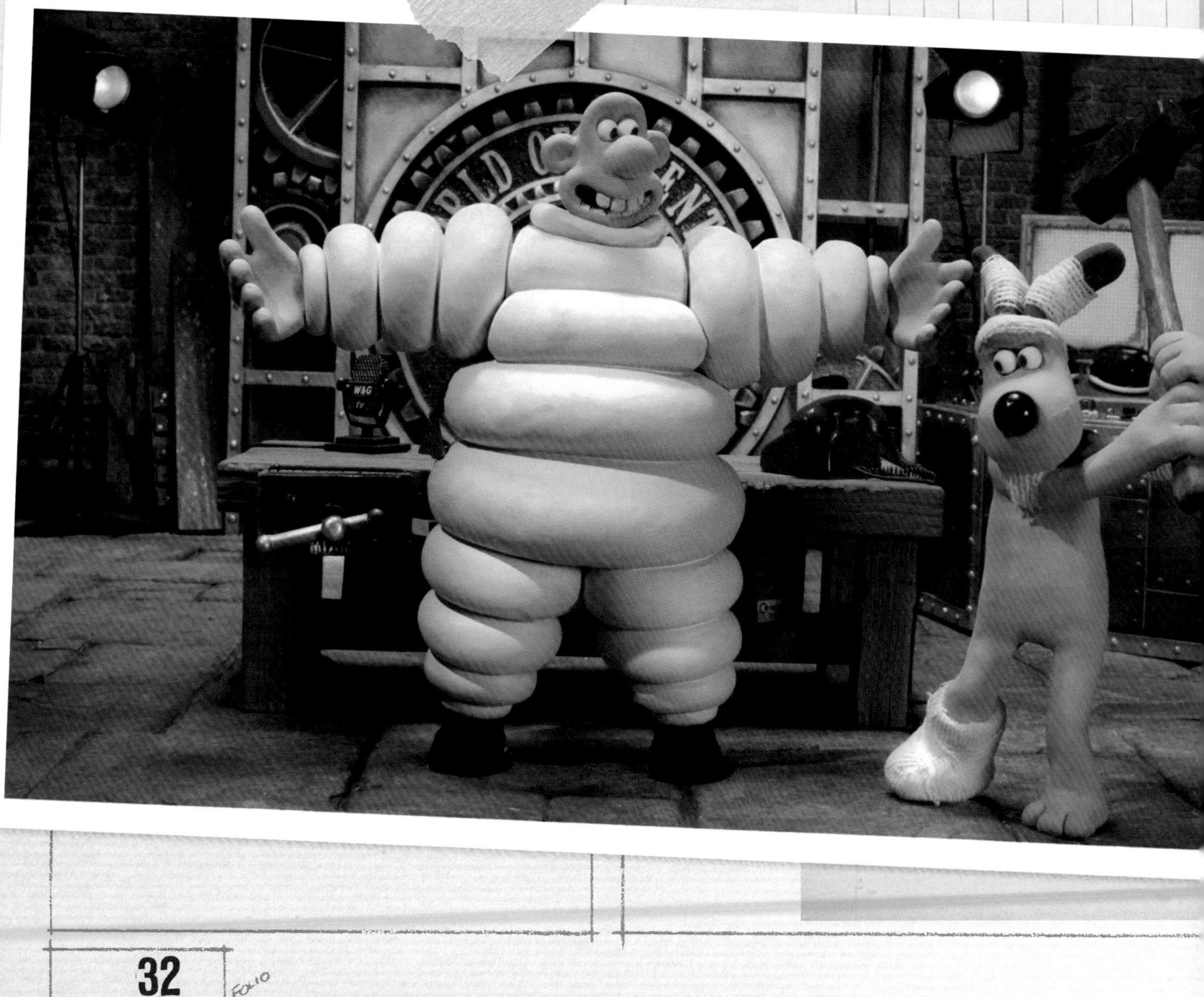
W&G

 FOLIO

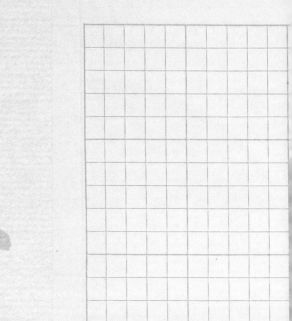

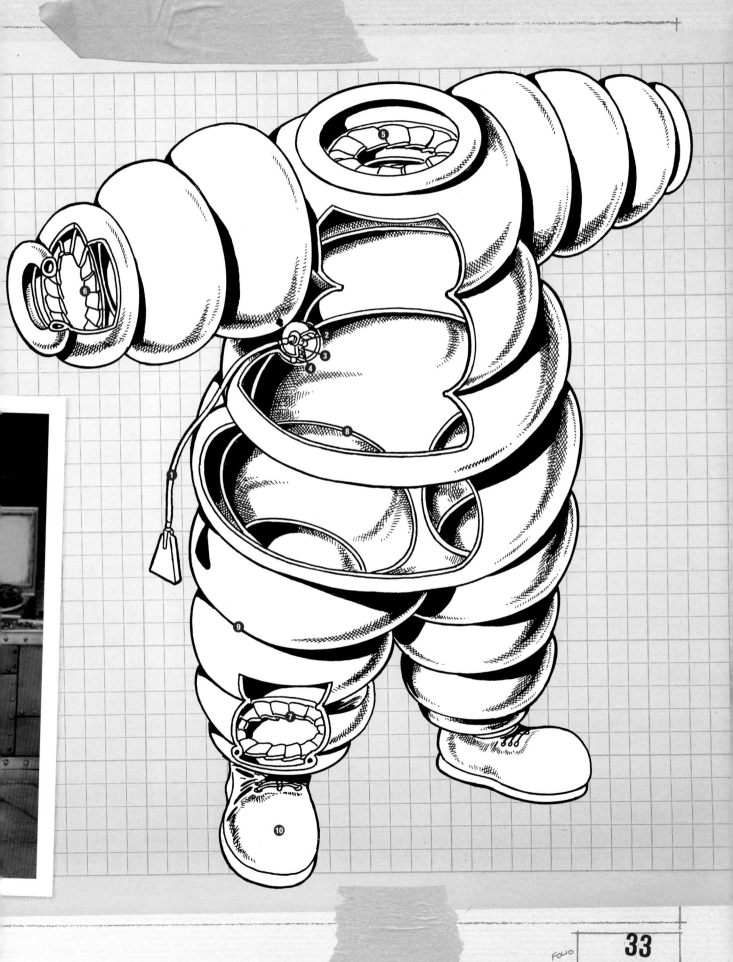

MAIN HEADING

MAIN PICTURE

BOWL-O-MATIC

Contents

CONTENTS LIST

PAGE NO.

SUB HEADING

General description

BODY COPY

DROP CAP

The Bowl-O-Matic is a fully integrated, shoulder-mounted cricket ball launcher, and is intended to take the strain out of bowling for cricketers at all levels. At the same time, ball delivery is improved and, hopefully, more wickets taken. Its functional design is based on the principles of speed, accuracy and ease of use, making it equally at home on the club pitch or village green.

The chassis of the Bowl-O-Matic is a hollow wooden beam on top of which is mounted the main catapult apparatus, trajectory upper control rod and targeting array. Inside the beam is the trigger mechanism, the main components of which are a trigger, trigger tension spring, lower control rod and a launch activation hook and pivot.

The type of ball delivery is pre-set using the ball trajectory control dial, which is linked to the trigger mechanism via the upper control rod. The settings available are Leg break, Off break, Yorker and Googly. As the trigger is pulled, the launch activation hook is released via the lower control rod according to geometry determined by the position of the upper control rod. In short, the system fine tunes the point at which the catapult is released, which in turn determines the type of ball delivery.

Upon release, the launch arm is catapulted forward, relieving the tension in the catapult spring and releasing the ball at the optimum angle.

The Bowl-O-Matic comes equipped with a fixed magnification targeting array, which is mounted at the front of the device. This enables the appropriate bowling style to be determined in relation to the batsman and prevailing conditions.

The substantial trigger hand grip and padded shoulder rest act as braces against the recoil of the device, which can be vigorous. Even so, some discomfort may still be caused after prolonged use.

FOLIO

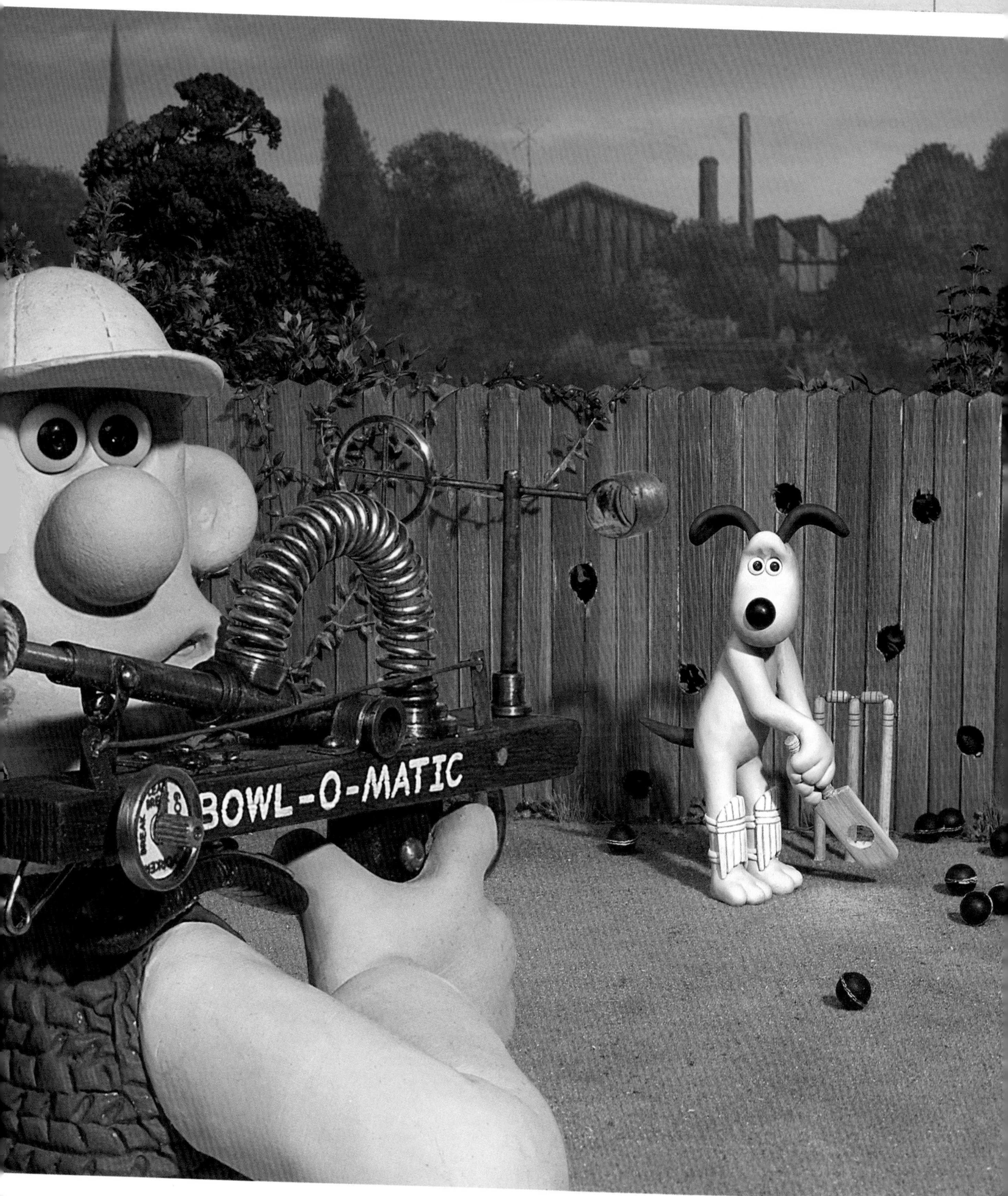
BOWL-O-MATIC

SUB HEADING

Bowl-O-Matic

CUTAWAY HERE

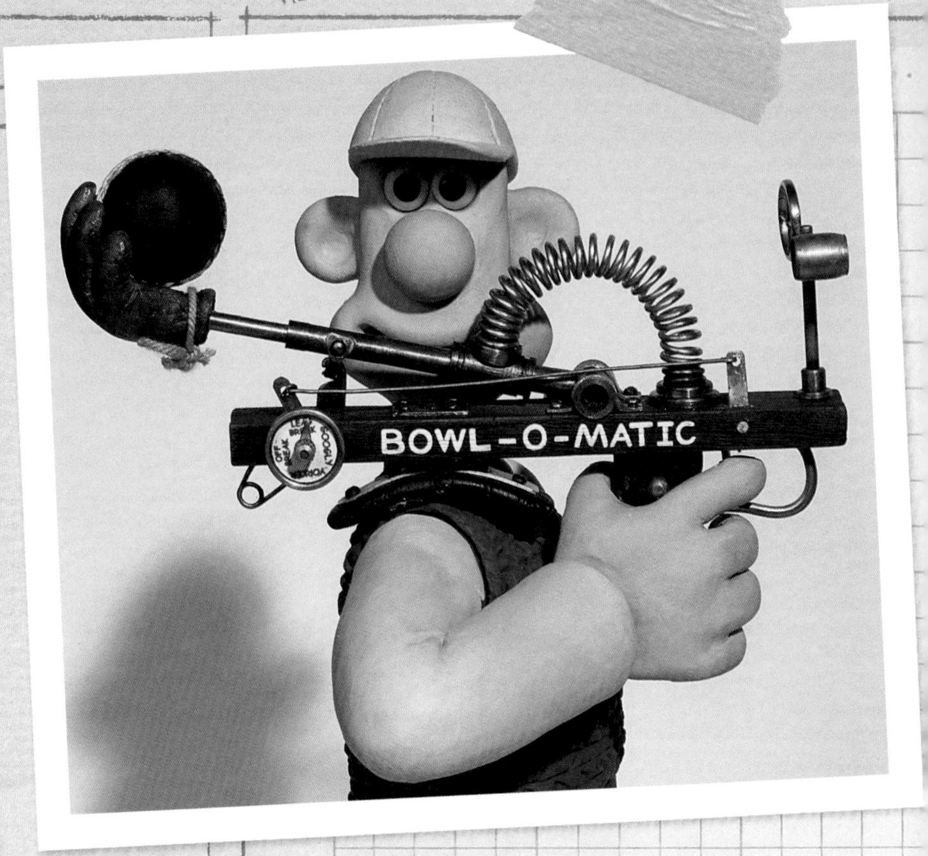

BOWL-O-MATIC

BULLET LIST

1. Cricket stump targeting array swivels to provide magnified viewfinder if desired.
2. Twin-lens fixed magnification target finder.
3. Bowl-O-Matic bodywork constructed from hollowed-out wooden beam.
4. Cricket ball.
5. Super-efficient cricket ball catapult grip designed to replicate a bowler's hand.
6. Catapult cricket ball launch arm.
7. Catapult spring.
8. Trigger.
9. Trigger tension spring.
10. Forward pivoted rod control lever.
11. Trigger-activated upper control rod determines the style of bowling via the ball trajectory control dial.
12. Rear pivoted rod control lever.
13. Launch activation hook pivot.
14. Launch activtion hook.
15. Lever tension spring.
16. Trigger-activated lower control rod located inside the Bowl-O-Matic operates the launch activation hook, which in turn releases the catapult arm.
17. Ball trajectory control dial.
18. Control dial programming knob.
19. Padded shoulder rest.
20. Reinforced hand grip enables operator to brace for recoil.

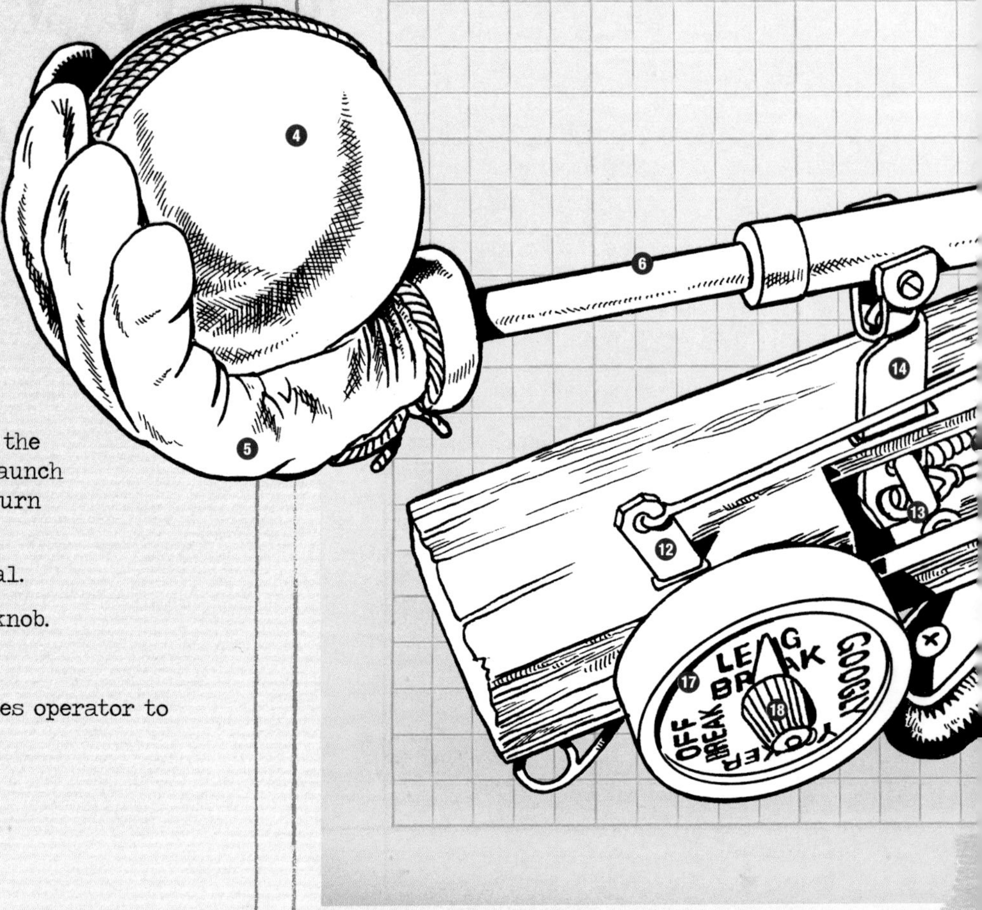

4
6
14
5
13
12
LEG BREAK
GOOGLY
YOKER
OFF BREAK
17
18

FOLIO

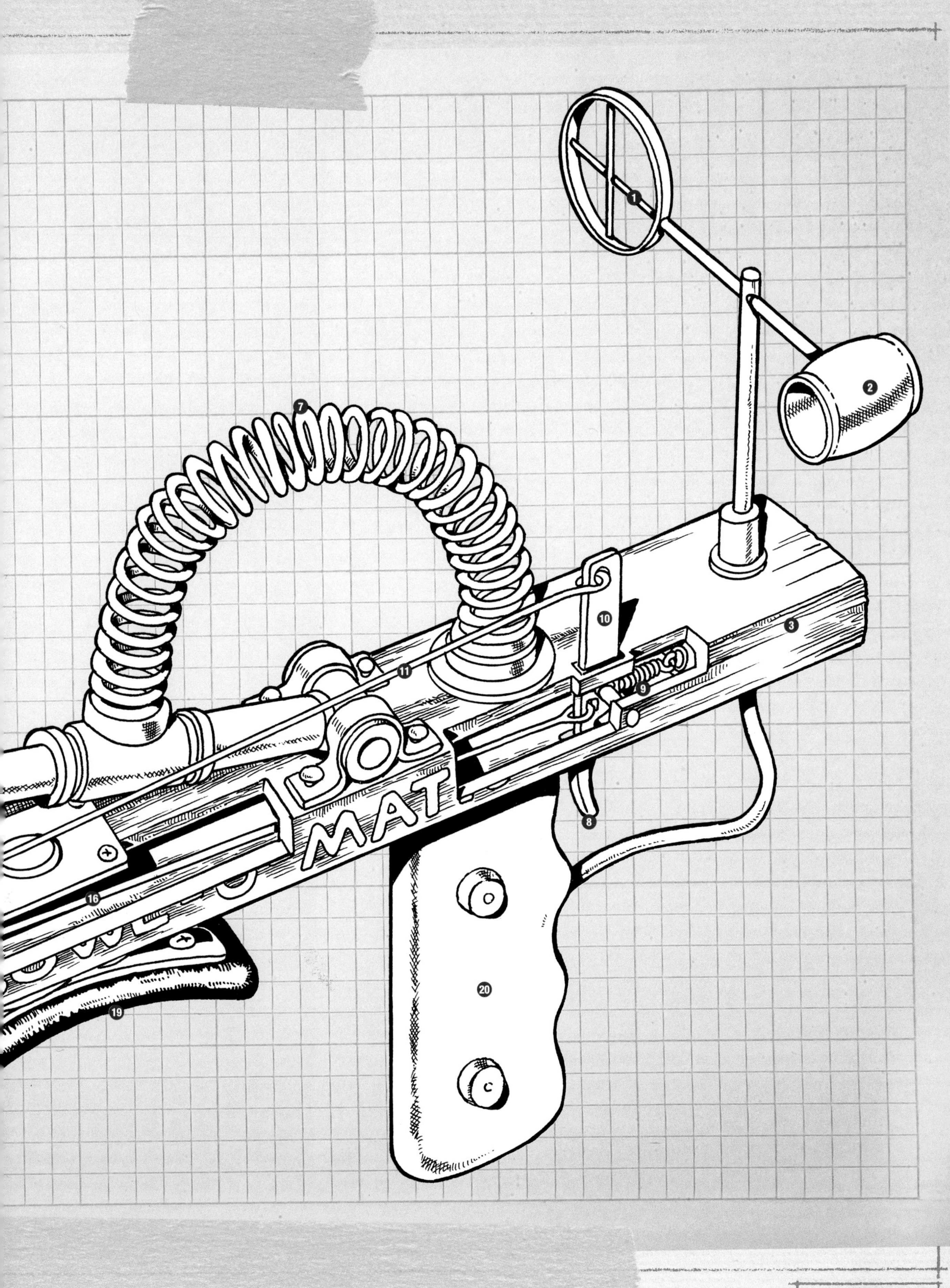
1
2
3
7
8
9
10
11
16
19
20
MAT

MAIN HEADING

HOVER WELLIES

SUB HEADING

Contents

SUB HEADING

General description

BODY COPY

DROP CAP

Whether employed as a safety device for use when encountering deep puddles, or as general transport across land, water, snow and ice, the Hover Wellies are an elegant addition to every inventor's wardrobe.

Each Hover Welly is an oversized Wellington boot onto which is fitted a substantial air intake above the toe section. Inside the intake housing is an electric motor, which is powered by a battery. The motor drives a four-bladed fan, mounted horizontally inside the intake housing on a support spanning its diameter. The fan sucks air in through a safety grille on top of the intake housing and forces it into a pair of curved ducts running either side of the wearer's foot. The forced air passes through the ducts and down through holes in the sole of the boot where it fills a compartmentalised air bag. Holes between the compartments ensure that the air bag is filled evenly so that it becomes rigid while remaining flexible over rough surfaces. Slits in the base of the air bag permit the air to escape under high pressure, thus creating a cushion of air, which lifts the boot just clear of the ground. The wearer of the Hover Wellies is now free to move around on any surface.

Forward propulsion is provided by a three-bladed propeller on each boot, driven by an electric motor, which is enclosed in a nacelle and mounted on a support at the rear of the boot. On top of each nacelle is a master on/off switch controlling both the lift fan and the rear propeller.

Internal padding and a fleece lining ensure a snug fit and comfort for the user in all weather conditions. A battery is housed in a compartment at the rear of each boot and is accessed from the inside via a padded flap. Therefore, battery replacement requires boot removal.

MINIATURE

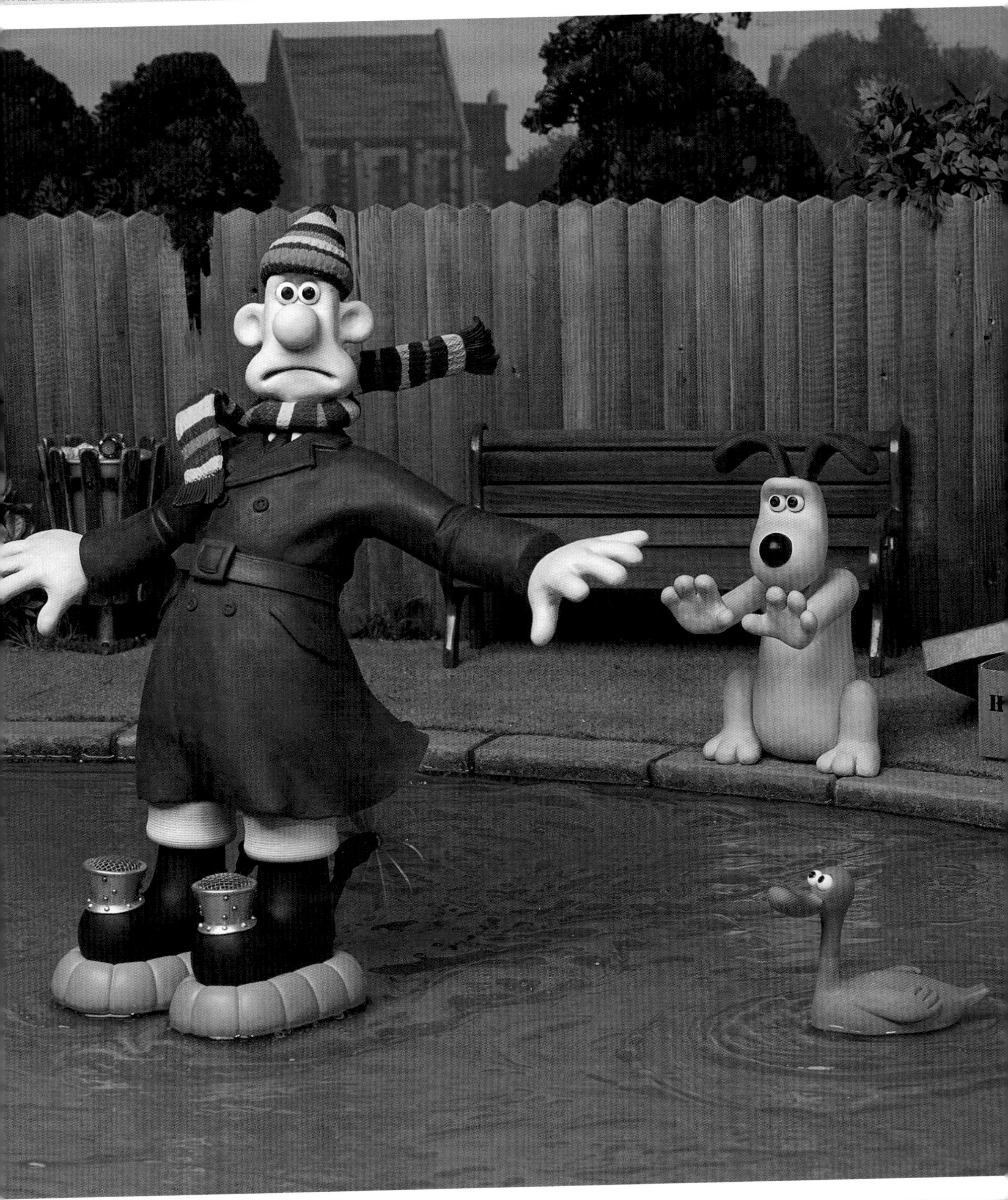

SUB HEADING

Hover Wellies

BULLET LIST

1. Air intake and fan housing.
2. Air intake safety grille prevents large items being sucked into fan housing.
3. Four-bladed fan provides lift.
4. Fan electric motor.
5. Power cable linking fan motor to battery.
6. Air ducts connecting fan housing to air bag below each boot. The operator's toes fit snuggly between each pair of ducts.
7. Compartmentalised air bag provides strength and stability when in use on all surfaces.
8. Slits in the base of each air bag create an air cushion for lift.
9. Battery flap button.
10. Battery in shoe heel provides power for both lift fan and rear propeller.
11. Propeller assembly mounting plate and battery housing.
12. Power cable linking propeller motor to battery.
13. Propeller electric motor.
14. Rear-mounted propeller provides forward propulsion.
15. On/off switch built into top of propeller nacelle.

1
2
3

HOVERWEL
PROTOTYP

FOLIO

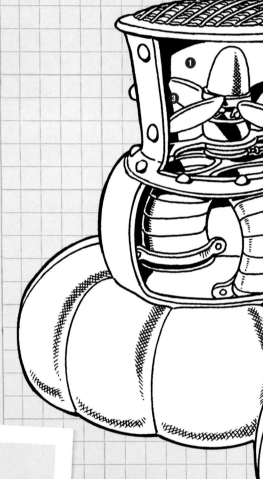

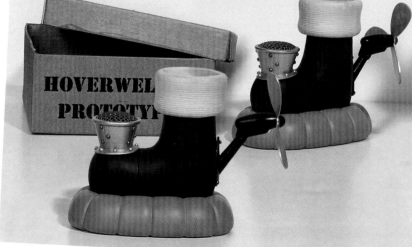

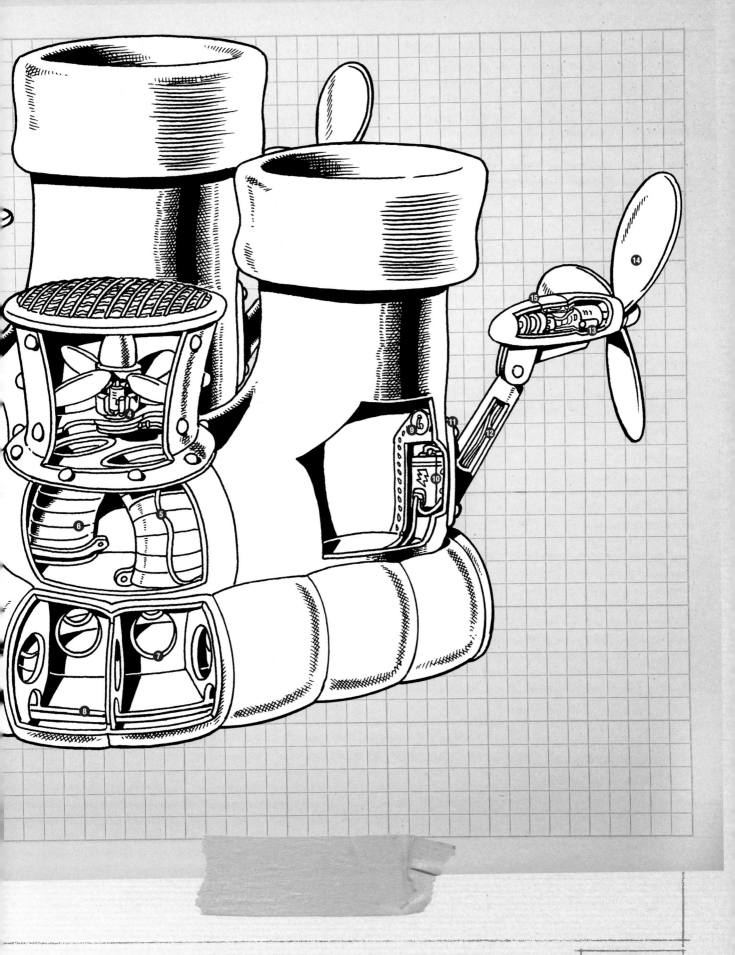

MAIN HEADING

GIRO BROLLY

MAIN PICTURE

SUB HEADING

Contents

CONTENTS LIST

PAGE NO.

SUB HEADING

General description

BODY COPY

DROP CAP

The Giro Brolly is designed to satisfy the needs of today's busy commuter as well as the more casual umbrella user. It provides not only a degree of protection from bad weather but also, and ingeniously, a means of motorised personal air transport.

When not in use, the device may be carried discreetly, appearing to unknowing passers-by much like any folded umbrella, albeit a bulky one. Also, like any full-size umbrella, it can function as a walking stick and as a pointer for drawing people's attention to points of interest while strolling.

However, upon deployment, it becomes clear that this is no ordinary umbrella. The Giro Brolly features a distinctive spiral hood, shaped to deflect rain and wind away from the user during inclement weather conditions. The design of the hood incorporates a number of features that prevent it from being blown inside out in high winds. These features alone render the Giro Brolly instantly superior to its conventional counterpart.

Once the hood is unfolded, the second feature of the device is revealed. A small yet extremely powerful electric motor is fitted into a lightweight hub casing just above the curved handle. The battery-operated motor powers a driveshaft, which runs through the telescopic support column at the centre of the Giro Brolly's hood. The driveshaft causes the hood to rotate and, by virtue of its unique helical design, acts as an 'air screw', thus lifting the entire assembly, and its user, into the air. The motor hub remains stationary relative to the rotating driveshaft, as does the umbrella handle and the user.

A few simple controls on the motor hub allow the user to start and stop the motor and control ascent and descent as required. Directional control is, however, a little more unpredictable, particularly so in high wind conditions. Should the motor stop working, or the battery become discharged, the device enters failsafe mode whereby the user simply 'parachutes' to the ground, hopefully landing somewhere near a bus stop.

FOLIO

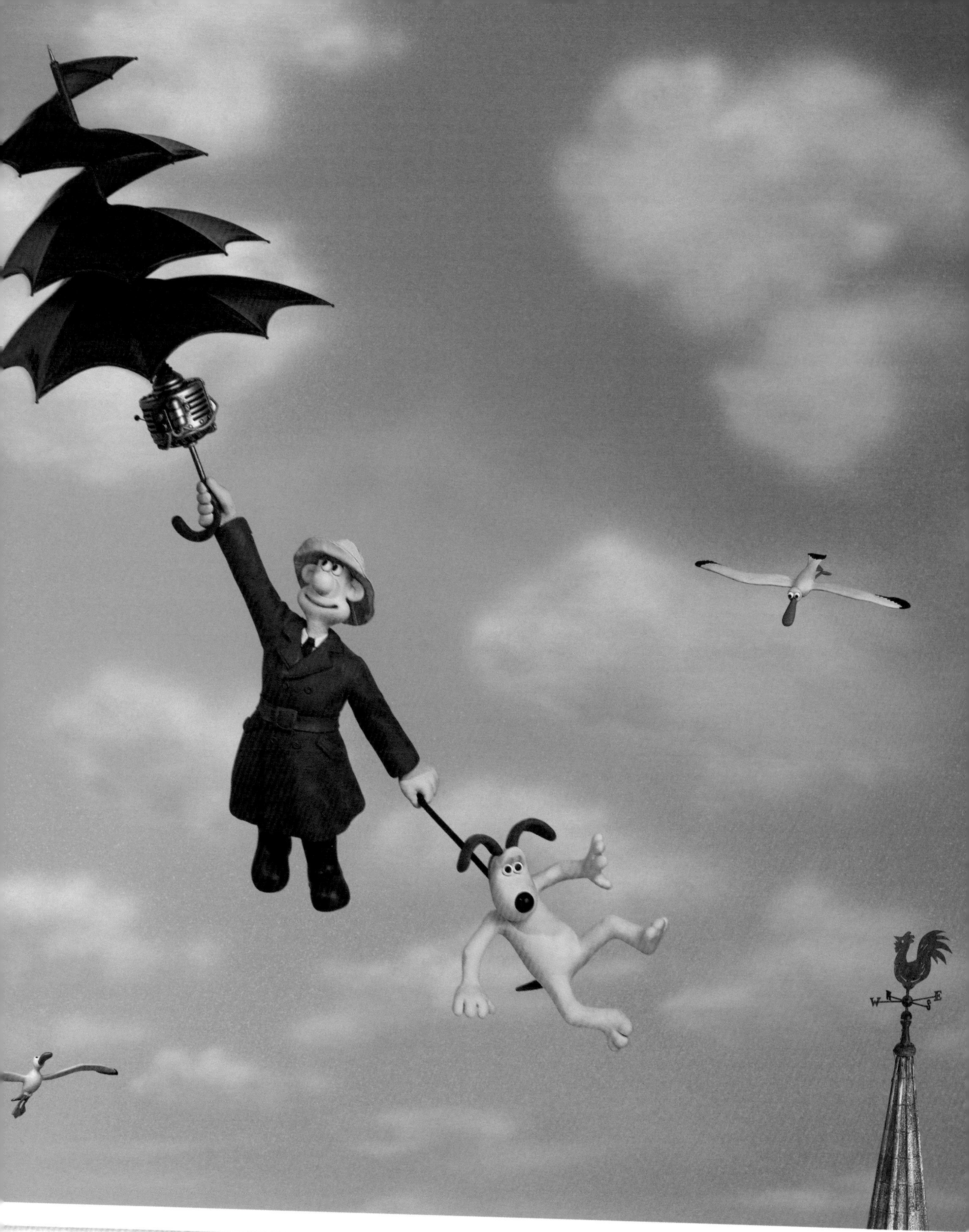

SUB HEADING

CUTAWAY HERE

Giro Brolly

POWER

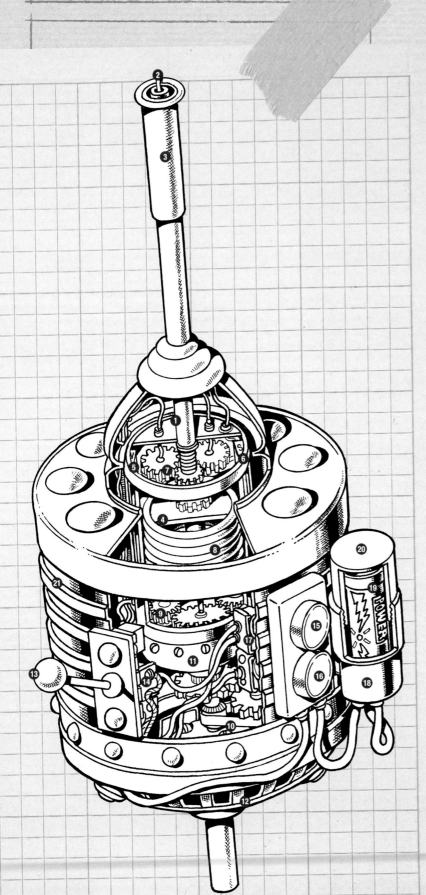

1. Umbrella internal deployment rod.
2. Deployment rod control line.
3. Drive shaft.
4. Wire coil support armature.
5. Stator permanent magnet.
6. Reversed stator permanent magnet.
7. Armature control gearing.
8. Armature wire coil.
9. Drive shaft speed control gearing.
10. Speed control gearing belt drive.
11. Cooling fan enclosure.
12. Cooling fan lower heat outlet grille.
13. Controlled ascent/descent lever.
14. Switching circuitry.
15. On/off power switch.
16. Umbrella deployment switch.
17. Switching circuitry.
18. Battery compartment.
19. Long-life battery.
20. Screw-top battery compartment lid.
21. Motor heat dissipation grille.
22. Dual-purpose umbrella hood prevents the user getting wet in inclement conditions and provides lift for flight when rotated.
23. Aerodynamically shaped spar tips for balanced flight.
24. Telescopic hood support column.
25. Powerful electric motor controls umbrella 'blade' rotation speed.
26. Super-grip umbrella handle.

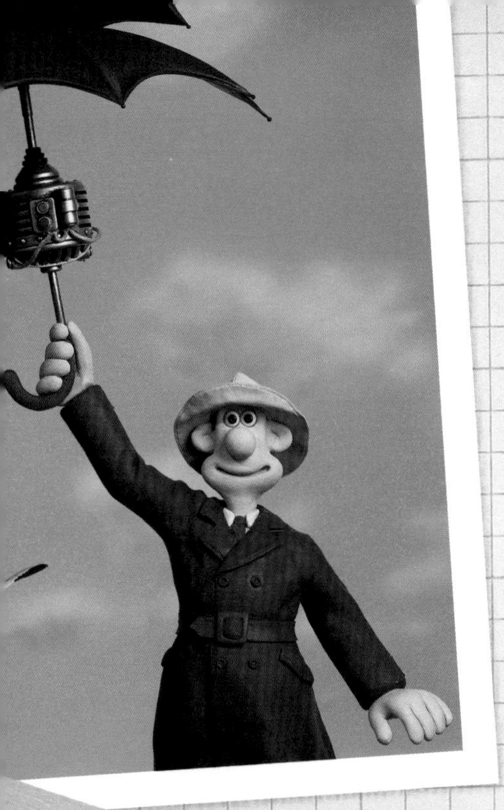

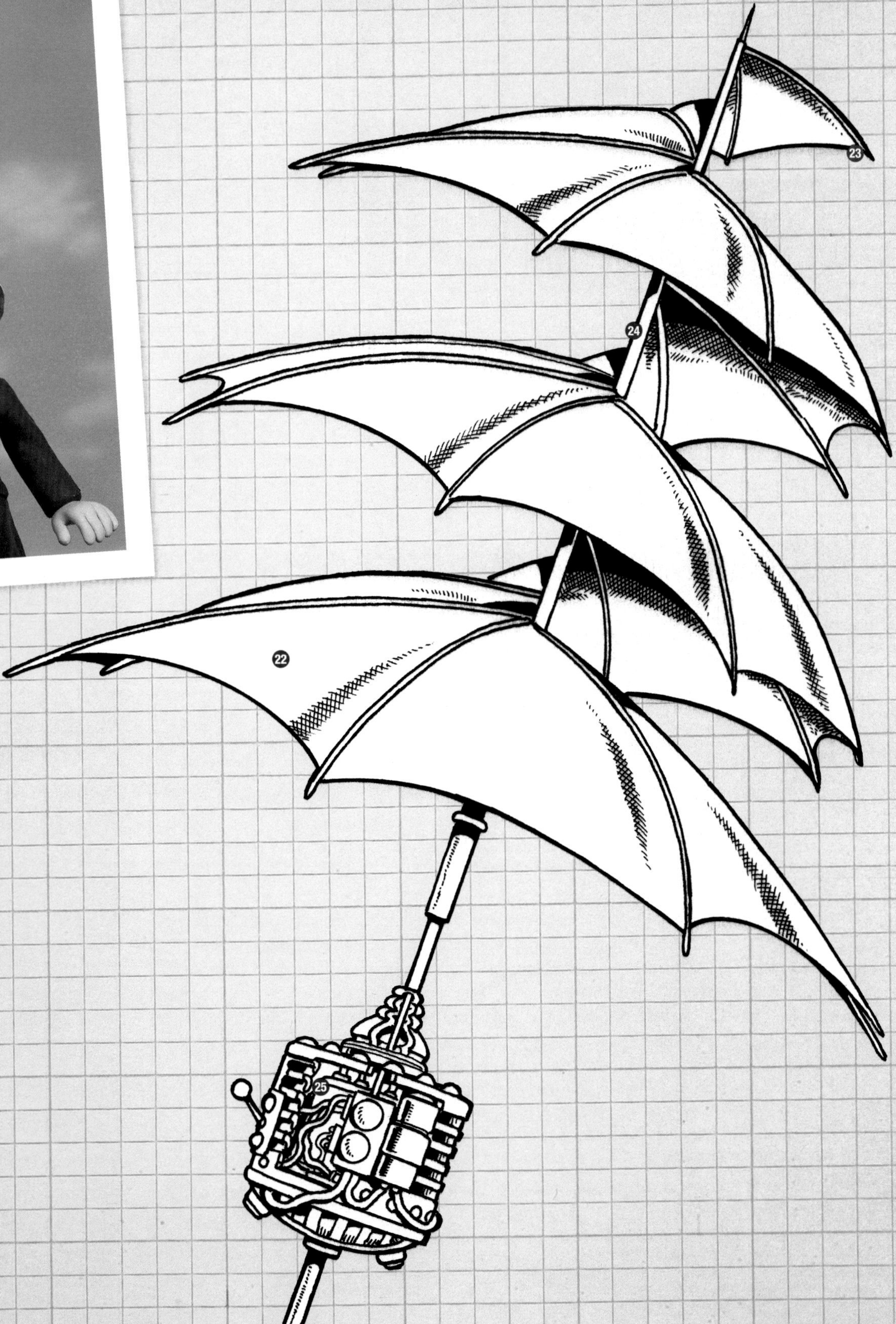

23
24
22
25
26

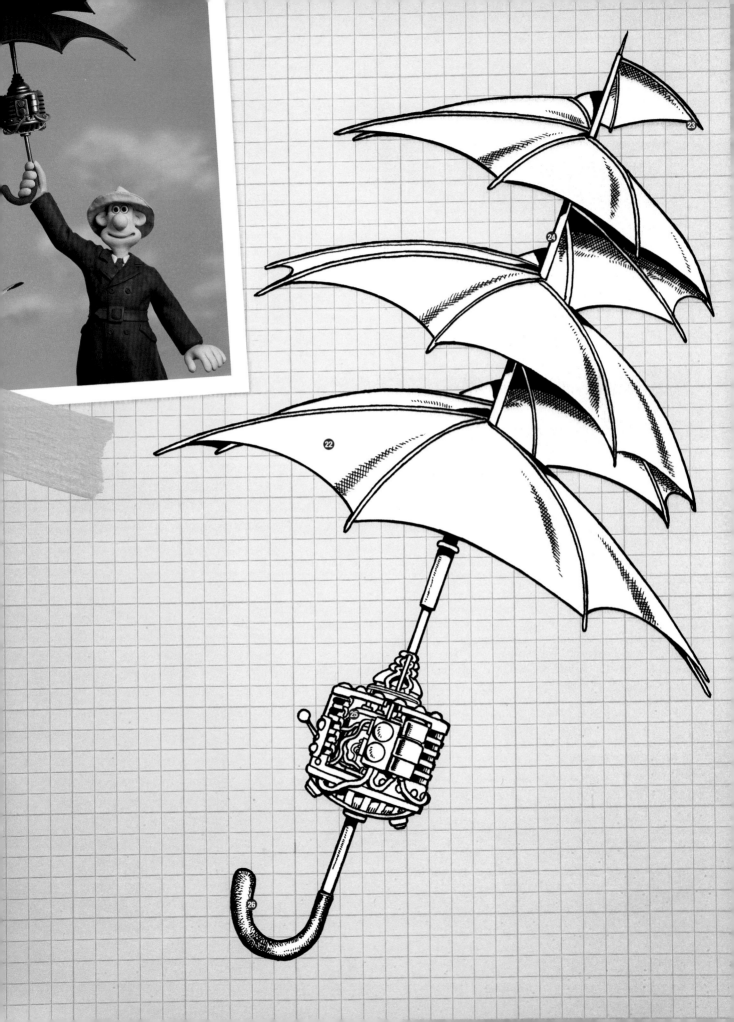

MAIN HEADING

Mk-1 EASY IRON

SUB HEADING

General description

BODY COPY

DROP CAP

The Mk-1 Easy Iron is designed to partially automate and greatly speed up the arduous task of ironing shirts, trousers and tank tops (the device could also be used to iron a full range of other garments, subject to further testing).

The main apparatus consists of a heat-resistant conveyor belt (the ironing board), which is driven by an operator (Wallace) by pedal power through a system of chains and gears. The ironing part is performed by two irons, which are strapped to the feet of an assistant (Gromit). The pedal operator selects the speed of the conveyor, depending on the type of garment to be ironed. He then places the garment on the conveyor, which carries it towards the ironing assistant, who then 'skates' over it with the irons strapped to his feet.

The irons themselves are attached to the assistant's feet by adjustable leather straps. They are connected to standard household power sockets by extra-long, flexible cables, which are coiled to take up any slack during use.

Whereas a temperature dial is used to control the heat setting of a conventional iron, the Mk-1 Easy Iron relies on the speed that the garment travels along the conveyor and hence the amount of time it spends in contact with the irons, which are held at a constant temperature by a fixed thermostat control. Cotton shirts require a slow speed setting to allow time for the assistant to iron out all creases, not forgetting collars and cuffs, while woollen tank tops and silk ties require a fast speed setting to minimise contact time with the irons and, hence, the chances of burning.

The Mk-1 Easy Iron is not recommended for garments that traditionally require a very low heat setting (for example, nylon and acetate) unless the operator is prepared to pedal extremely quickly using the top speed setting.

MAIN PICTURE

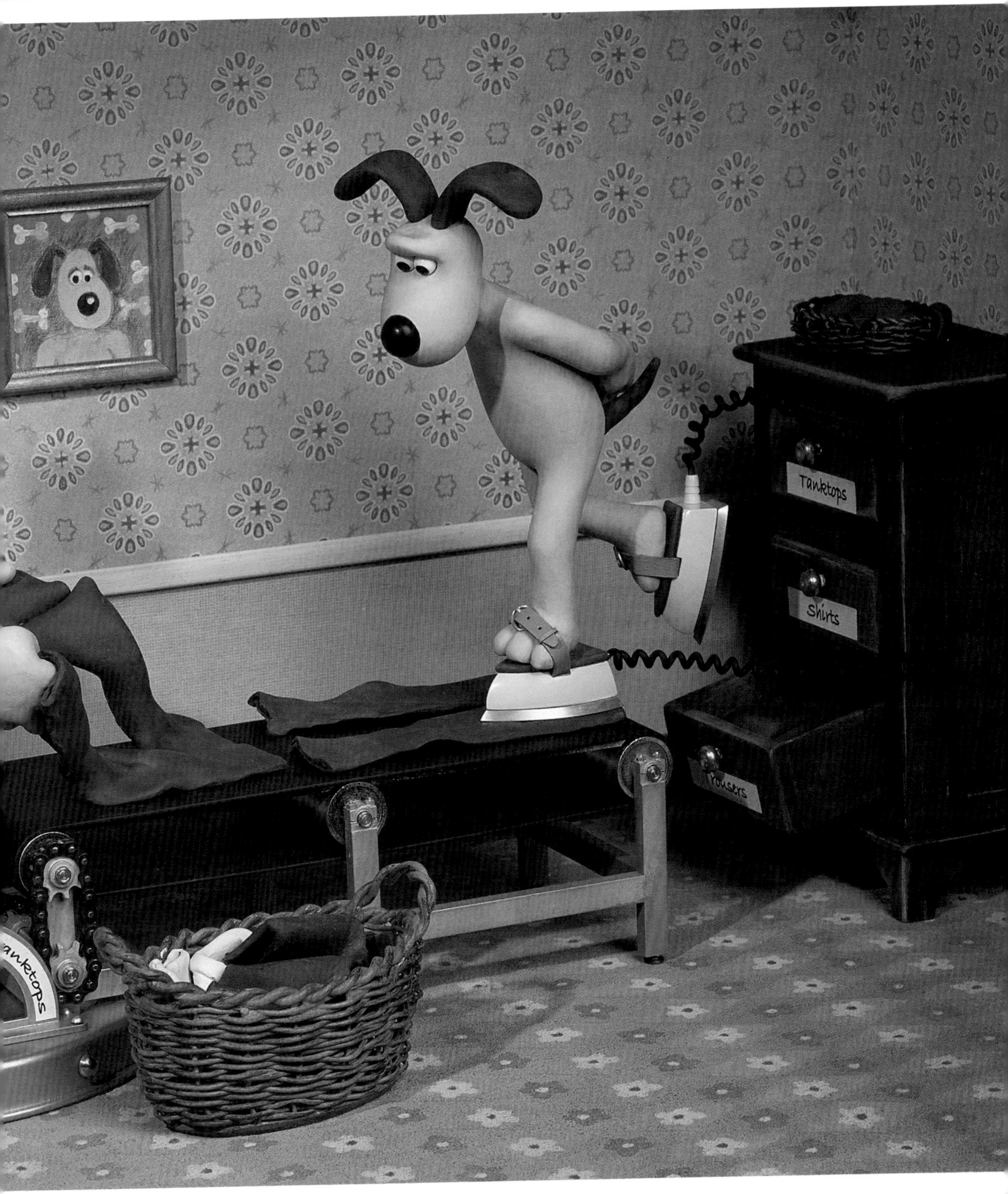
Tanktops
Shirts
Trousers
anktops

Mk–1
Easy Iron

Shirts
Trousers
Tanktops

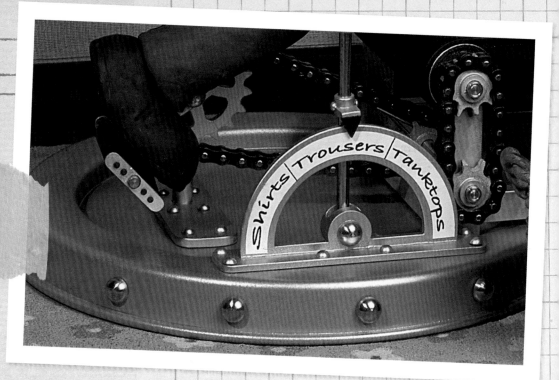

1. Heat-resistant ironing conveyor belt.
2. Conveyor frame strengthened to take Gromit's weight.
3. Chain drive wheel.
4. Foot pedals.
5. Ironing speed control gearing.
6. Ironing speed chain drive linked to pedal system.
7. Pedal operator's saddle.
8. Garment ironing selection lever is linked to chain drive and alters control gearing.
9. Iron.
10. Heat-resistant and cushioned foot pad prevents Gromit's feet from overheating.
11. Adjustable foot strap.
12. Flexible and insulated power cable.
13. Power points.
14. Ironing basket.
15. Three-drawer cabinet stores ironed tank tops, trousers and shirts.
16. Wicker basket for ties.

7
8
3
6
4
5
Shirts
Trousers
Tanktops

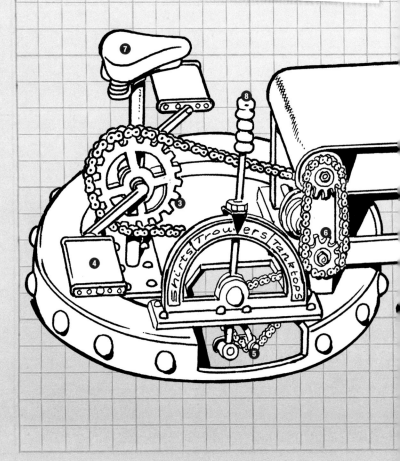

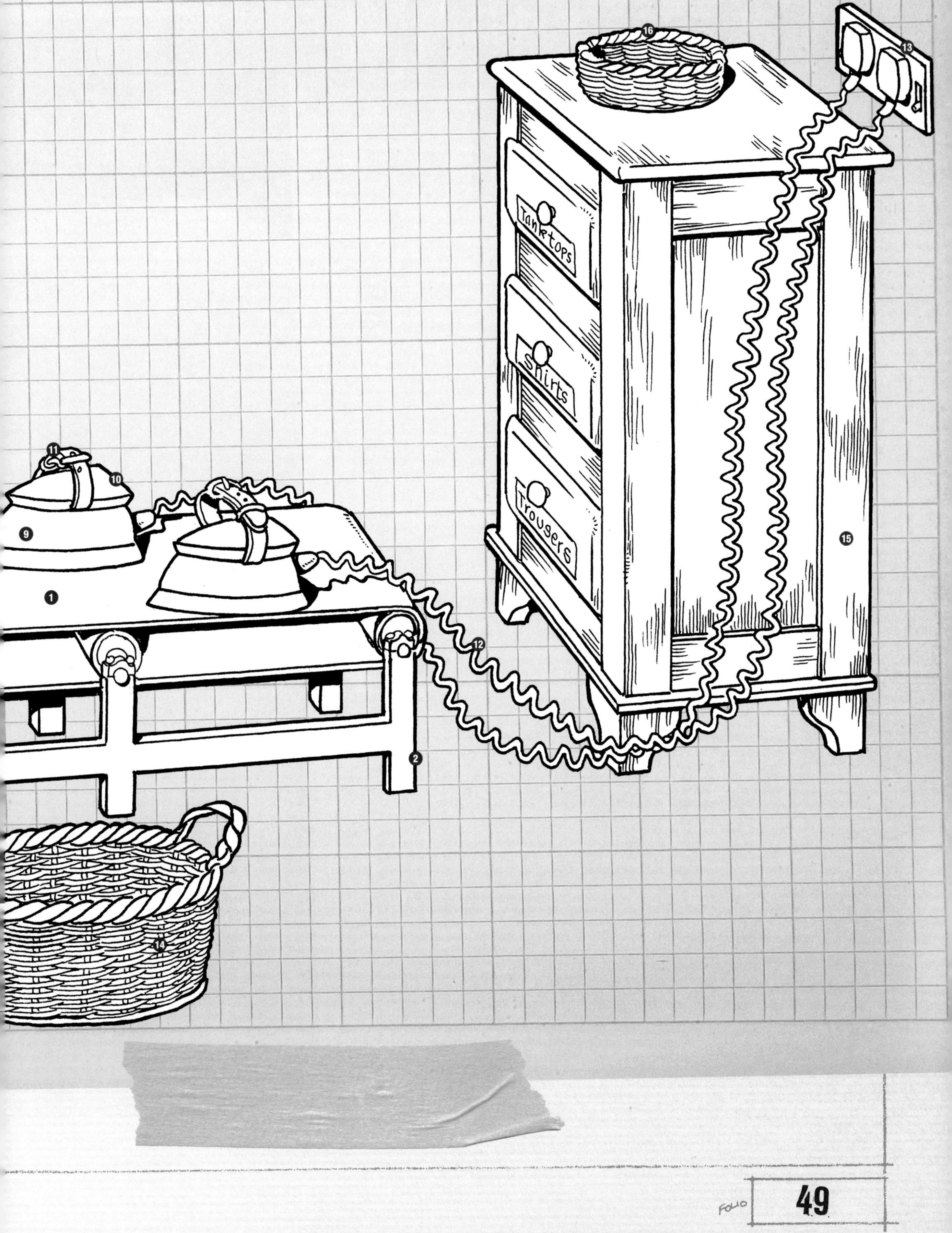
Tanktops
Shirts
Trousers
11
10
9
1
12
2
16
13
15
14

MAIN HEADING

FUEL & DRINKS DISPENSER

SUB HEADING

Contents

CONTENTS LIST

PAGE NO.

SUB HEADING

General description

BODY COPY

DROP CAP

The fuel and drinks dispenser pump used in Wallace and Gromit's Top Bun bakery business is one of those ideas that makes you wonder why no one has thought of it before. It is a compact and elegant solution to the refuelling needs of vehicles and staff in and around the workplace.

Based on a standard forecourt petrol pump, the device serves four-star and unleaded petrol plus diesel, which are all drawn from underground storage tanks by an impeller pump and passed through an air separator unit in the base of the unit. The type of fuel is pre-selected by pressing the appropriate button on the front panel of the machine. This activates a selection valve that determines the correct underground storage tank to draw from.

In the top of the unit three thermo-insulated containers are filled with tea, coffee and milk. These are connected via flexible tubes to a drink dispenser pump and selection valve, with selection again activated by buttons on the front of the machine. From here, the selected beverage (tea or coffee, with milk to taste) is pumped via the fuel meter before delivery.

The delivery volume of the selected fuel/beverage is measured by a two-piston meter and displayed on a fuel quantity indicator on the front panel of the machine. The fuel/beverage is then dispensed via the fuel hose and nozzle in the normal manner.

The nozzle is fitted with a hand-operated trigger and an automatic cut-off mechanism to prevent overfilling of fuel tank or mug. A display 'blimp' is mounted on top of the machine and illuminated when fuel and drinks are available.

 FOLIO

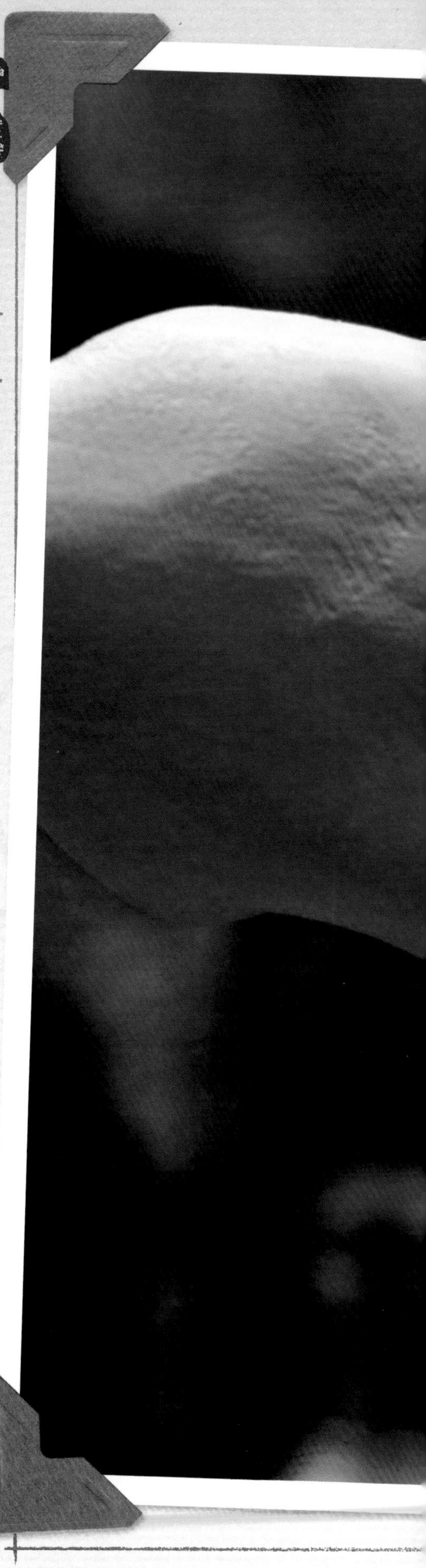

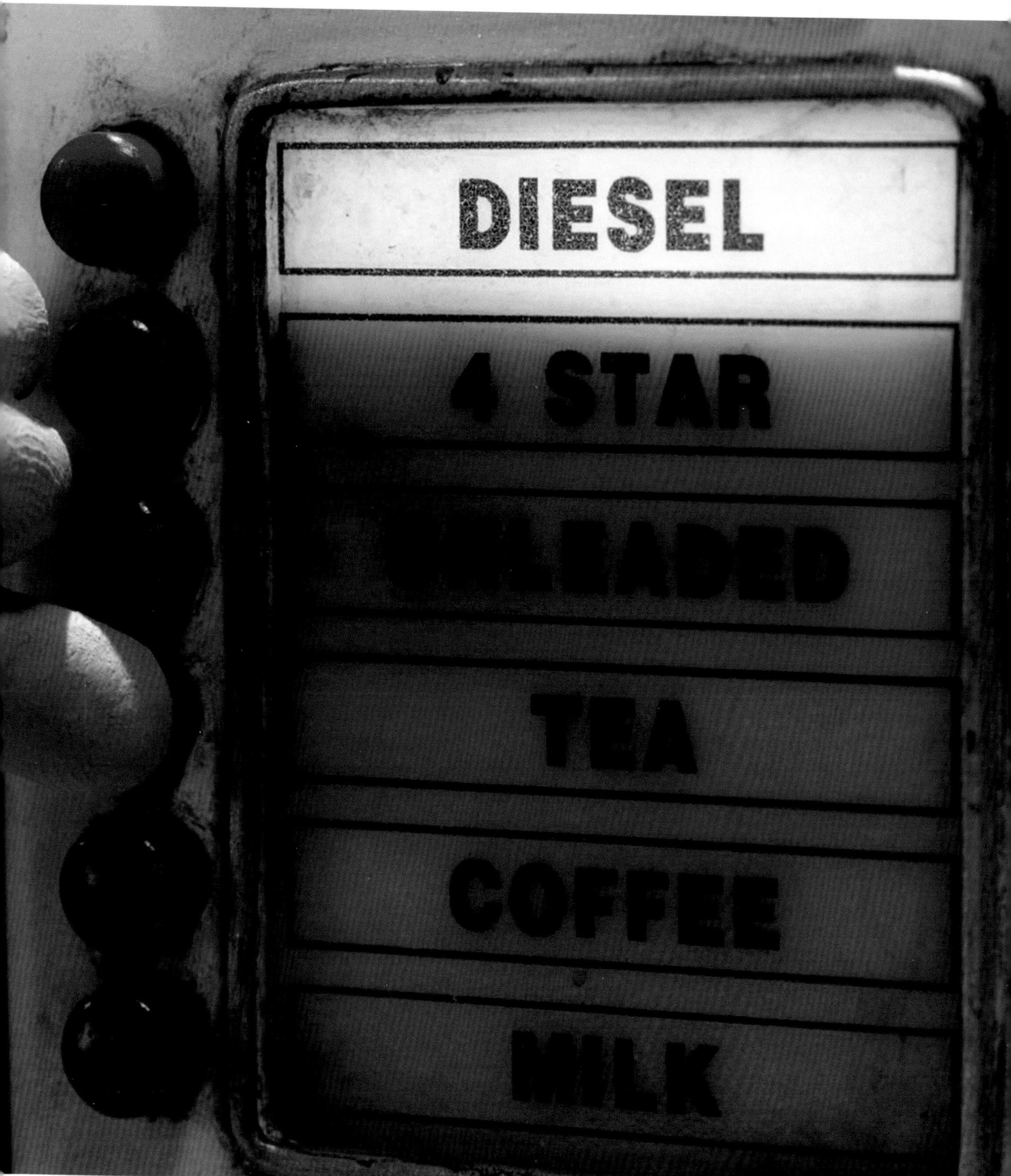
DIESEL
4 STAR
TEA
COFFEE

Fuel & Drinks Dispenser

❶ Fuel selection buttons.

❷ Backlit fuel selection indicators.

❸ Fuel indicator backlighting bulb and wiring.

❹ Fuel volume indicator.

❺ Nozzle for van fuel tank or appropriate tea/coffee mug.

❻ Starting handle for pump motor and fuel volume indicator motor.

❼ Hand-operated compression trigger controls flow of fuel. Automatic cut-off prevents overfilling.

❽ Fuel hose.

❾ Two-piston meter makes four revolutions for each gallon of fuel delivered.

❿ Pump draws fuel from underground tanks.

⓫ Pump impeller.

⓬ Fuel selection valve.

⓭ Air separator.

⓮ Diesel pipe.

⓯ 4 Star petrol pipe.

⓰ Unleaded petrol pipe.

⓱ Hose connects drinks dispenser pump and selection valve to main fuel system.

⓲ Heating element maintains temperature of tea or coffee.

⓳ Drinks dispenser pump and selection valve.

⓴ Thermo-insulated containers pre-filled each evening for use the next morning.

㉑ Drink refill caps.

㉒ Rear-mounted hose outlet.

㉓ Front panel hinges forward allowing maintenance access.

㉔ Wires to fuel pump display blimp internal lighting.

㉕ Fuel pump display blimp.

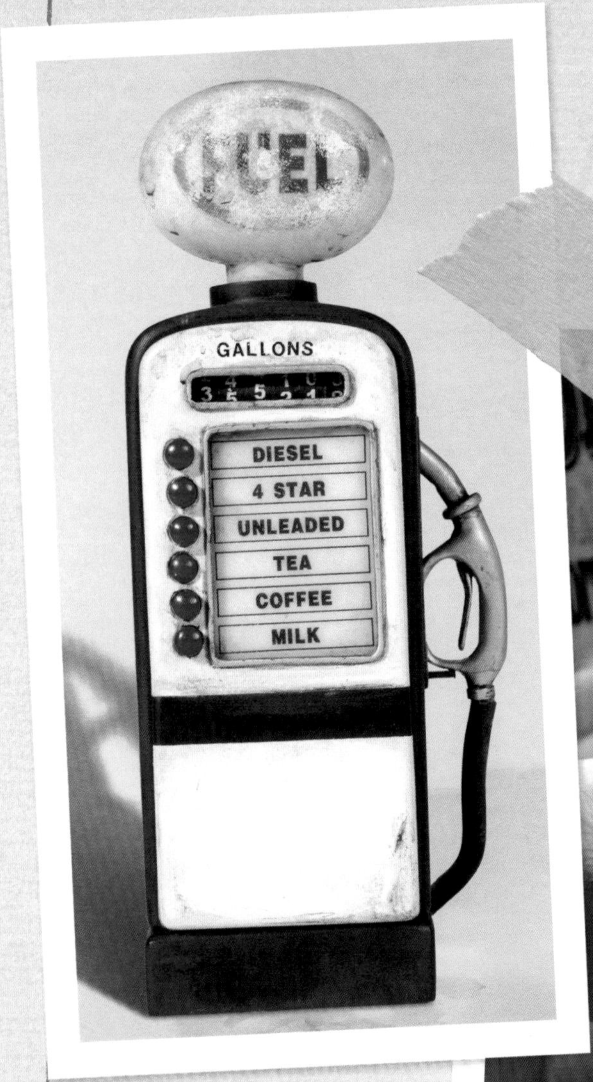
FUEL
GALLONS
DIESEL
4 STAR
UNLEADED
TEA
COFFEE
MILK

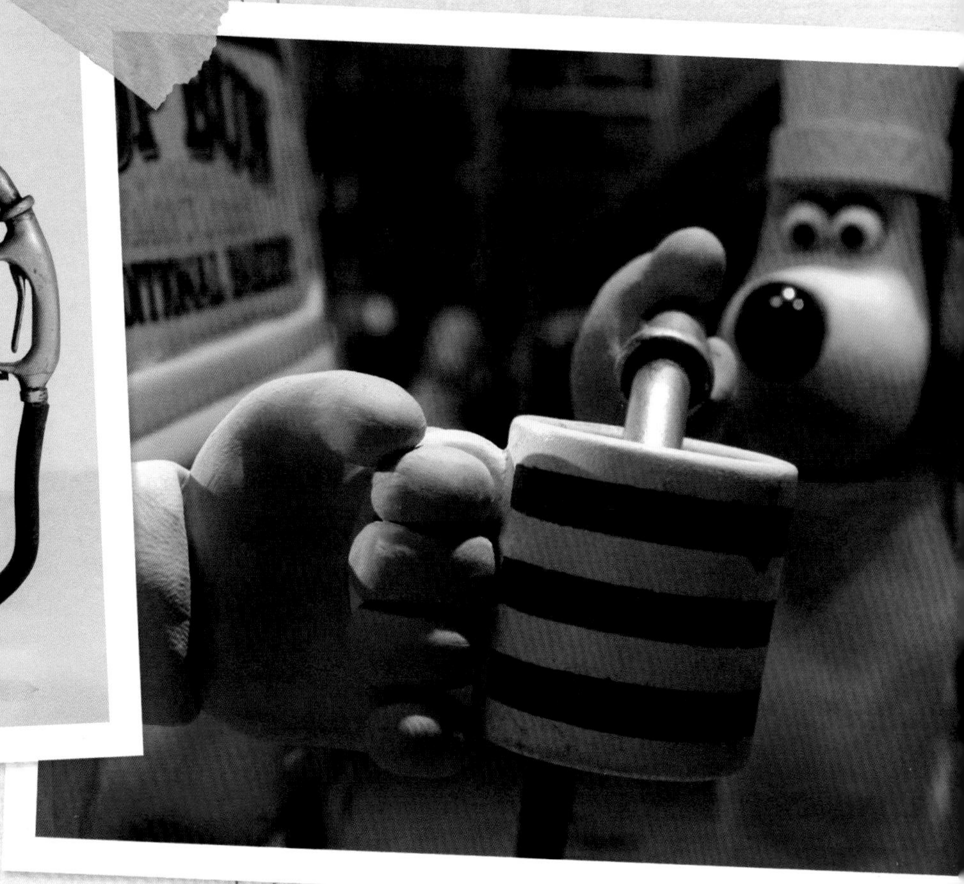

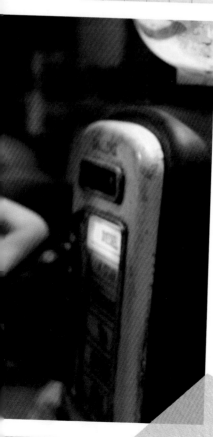

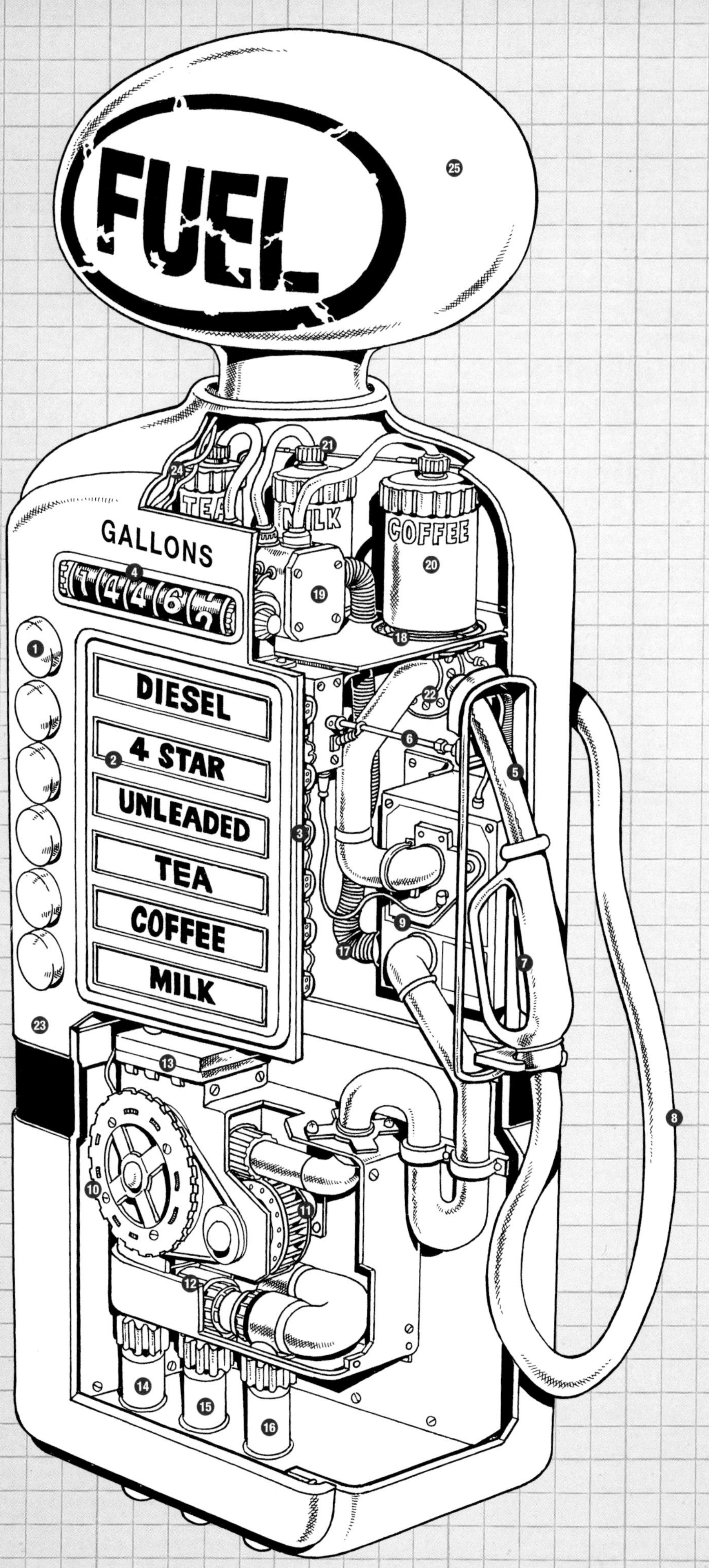
FUEL
GALLONS
DIESEL
4 STAR
UNLEADED
TEA
COFFEE
MILK
TEA
MILK
COFFEE

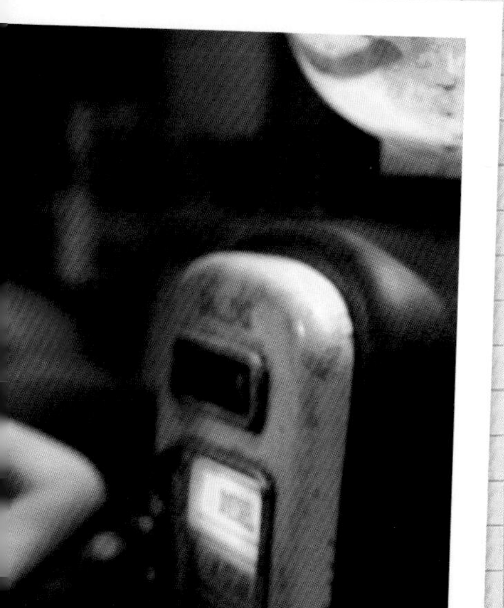

ANTI-PESTO LAUNCH SYSTEM

Contents

General description

One of Wallace and Gromit's more adventurous business schemes is 'Anti-Pesto', specialising in high-tech pest-control. The company offers a range of tailor-made services to deal with pests such as rabbits, rats and insects (but particularly rabbits), which threaten vegetable gardens and allotments, and cause torment for their nervous owners. The Anti-Pesto team (Wallace and Gromit) are especially skilled in the humane capture of rabbits, and they have developed a number of ingenious contraptions to lure, bait and trap them without harm. Many of these are simple and effective while some are considerably more elaborate. One such device is the 'Bun Vac 6000', which is covered in detail later in the book.

As the annual vegetable competition at Tottington Hall draws closer, local residents are becoming extremely anxious, and many are willing to go to great lengths to protect their potential prize-winning vegetables from vermin and unscrupulous rivals alike. The stakes are high and Anti-Pesto's services are in huge demand.

The Anti-Pesto 'Special Wardrobe and Tools' (SWAT) team is an elite pest-control operations unit, which is ready to respond quickly at any time to any pest emergency that arises. The gardens and greenhouses of Anti-Pesto's clients are protected by sophisticated intruder alarms and early-warning systems. Infrared and sonic motion sensors and expertly concealed surveillance cameras are just some of the devices employed to provide the ultimate in vegetable protection. These systems are all linked directly to Anti-Pesto's headquarters at 62 West Wallaby Street. Not only do they alert the SWAT team instantly of pest activity in the area but they also trigger the automatic launch system that can scramble the team within two minutes - even in the middle of the night.

The following pages describe the various elements of the launch system in step-by-step detail.

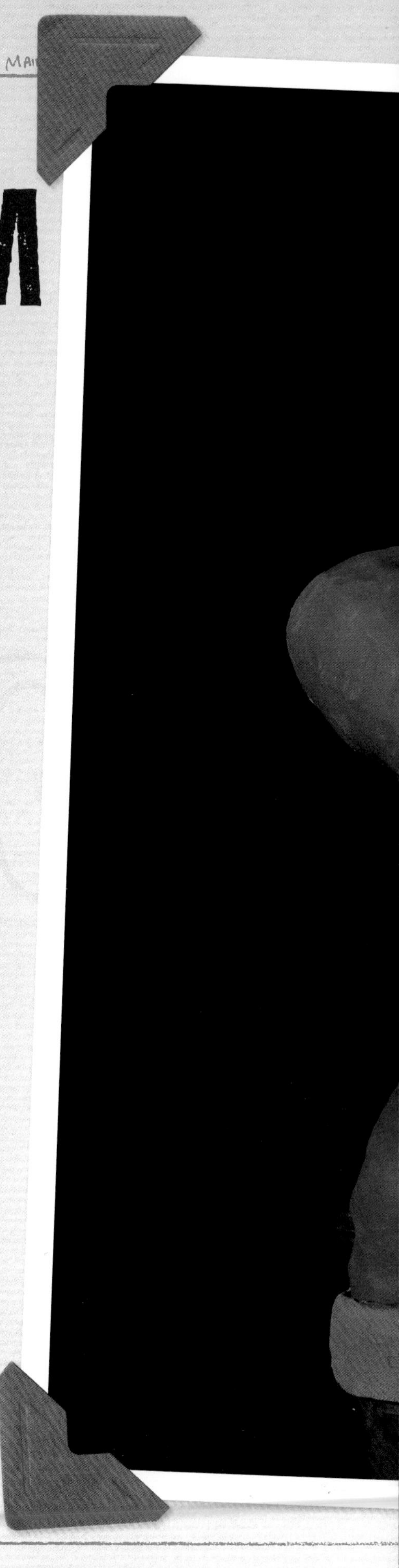

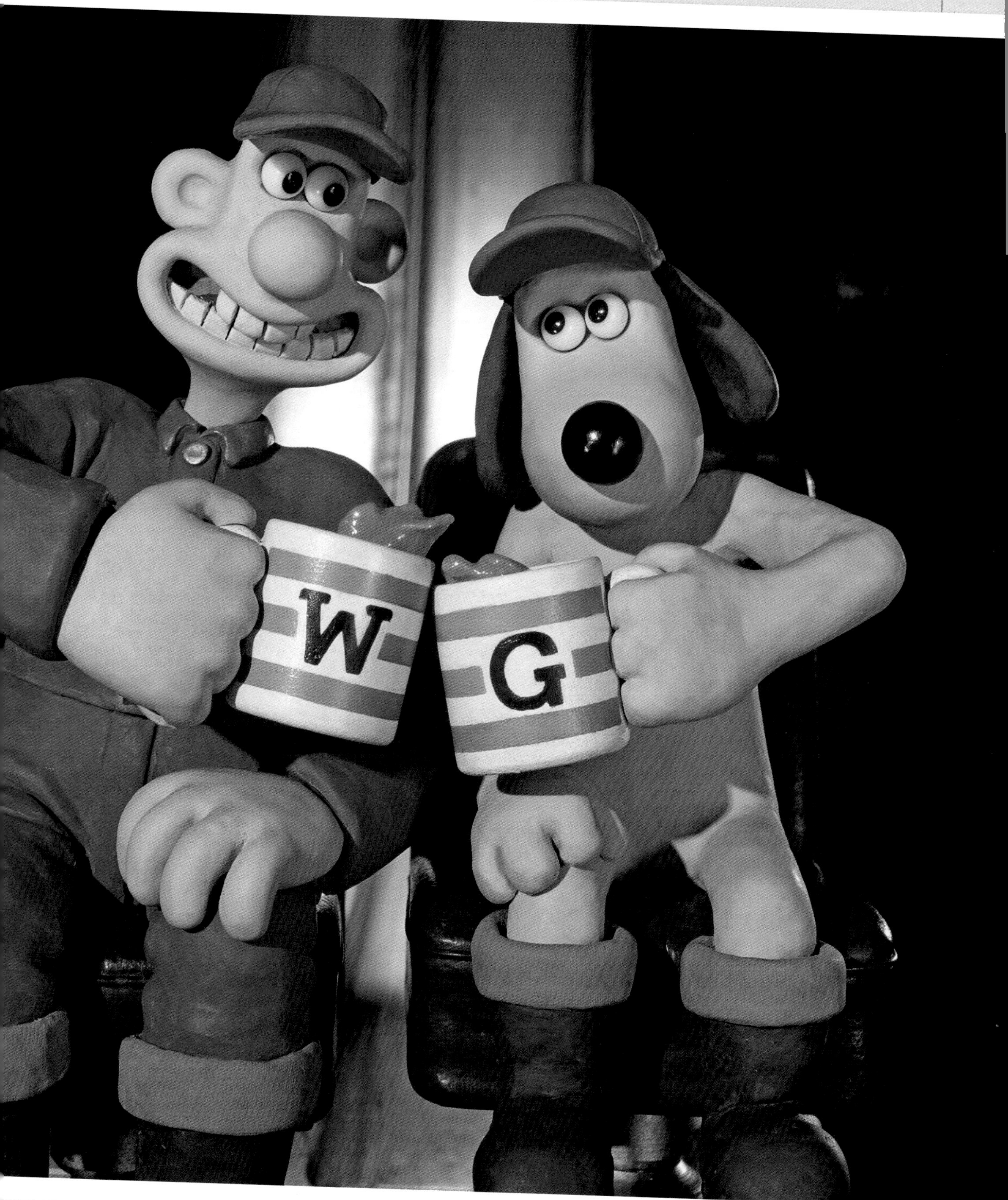
W
G

Anti–Pesto Launch System

1. A boiling kettle on the timer-controlled cooker begins the launch sequence.

2. Steam from the kettle turns the wall-mounted turbine.

3. The turbine is connected to a pulley and rocker, which activates the wake-up pole.

4. The wake-up pole wakes Gromit, just in time for phase two. …

5. The beds tip backwards through sliding panels in Wallace and Gromit's respective bedrooms.

6. Wallace and Gromit slide down the chutes, coming to rest head first. Their night caps are discarded by the impact.

7. Wallace and Gromit's caps are automatically fitted to their heads.

8. The bottom of the chute tips downwards, allowing Wallace and Gromit to continue their journey feet first.

9. Wallace and Gromit continue their journey down towards the catapult at the bottom of the cellar.

10. Once they 'land' in their waiting boots, cups of tea are supplied by the automated dispensers.

11. The catapult then swings round, ready for phase four. …

12. Once the catapult has swung round, activation grips pull the lower end towards the floor.

13. The grips are released, launching Wallace and Gromit into a double piked somersault as they approach the final section of the launch chute.

14. Wallace's downward motion allows him to don his overalls.

15. They continue their journey on the final section of the launch chute.

16. Wallace and Gromit come to rest on the folded down seats of the A35 Van at the bottom of the chute.

17. The seats and occupants are lifted on hydraulic rams up towards the waiting van in the garage above.

18. A hatch in the floor of the garage opens up to allow Wallace and Gromit to enter the van from below.

19. The seats enter the van via hatches in the floor and are secured in position by the seating support stanchions (see page 80) before the hydraulic rams retract and the two sets of hatches close.

20. The now-empty tea mugs are placed on retractable trays, and the van is ready to begin the 'Autostart' procedure using the crank handle (see page 80).

❶ Gas cooker with built-in timer switch (can also be activated by garden gnome alarm systems).

❷ Kettle.

❸ Wall-mounted steam turbine.

❹ Pulley and sprung rocker.

❺ Wake-up pole.

❻ Geared lifting mechanism pushes up through bedroom floor to tip bed backwards.

❼ Gromit's bed.

❽ Bed tipping hinge.

❾ 'Stinking Bishop' cheese.

❿ Cheese deployment arm.

⓫ Wallace's bed in upright 'Go' position.

⓬ Bed lifting mechanism.

⓭ Chute support beams.

⓮ Shoulder restraints prevent Wallace and Gromit from sliding any further.

⓯ Auto-cap deployment arms.

⓰ Chute direction auto-changer.

⓱ Extractor fan.

⓲ Cellar air-conditioning system.

⓳ Foul-air extraction pipes.

⓴ Top of launch system power plant

㉑ Launch system power plant.

㉒ Catapult activation arms, retracted into cellar/sub-basement floor space.

㉓ Catapult mechanics.

㉔ Tea maker One.

㉕ Tea maker Two.

㉖ Boots.

㉗ Power plant.

㉘ Catapult.

㉙ Catapult activation grips.

㉚ Wallace's overalls.

㉛ Chute leading to sub-basement beneath garage.

㉜ Sub-basement.

㉝ Van seats lie flat with the backs horizontal at the end of the chute so that Wallace and Gromit can slide directly onto them.

㉞ Retracted seating support stanchions.

㉟ Retractable tea mug trays.

㊱ Tea mug tray retraction arm power unit.

㊲ Back wall of garage.

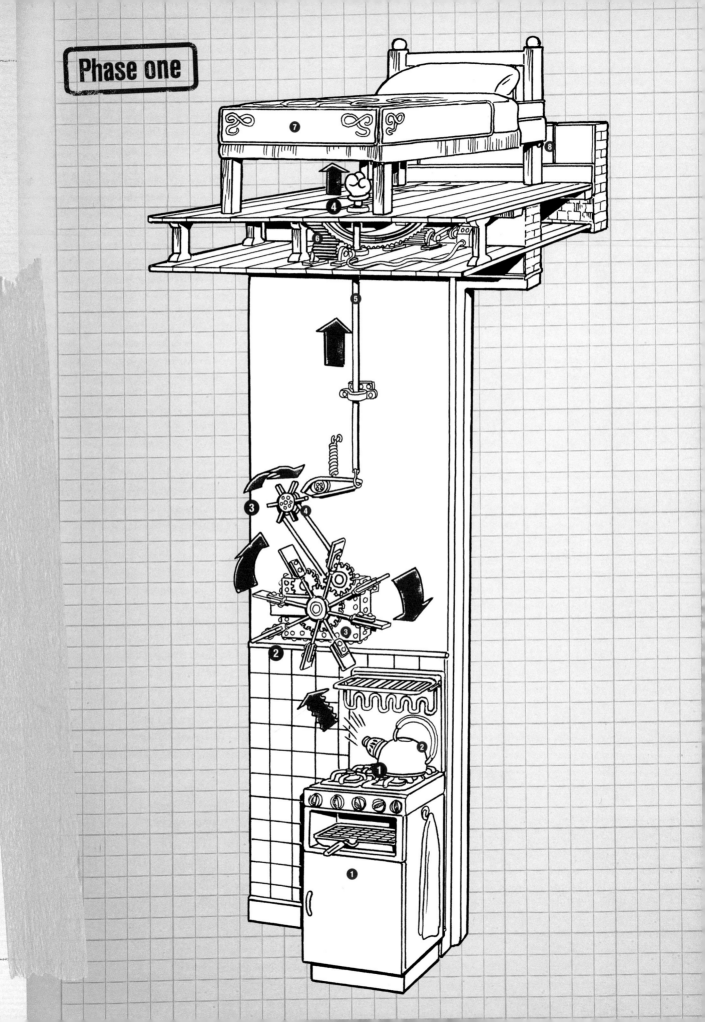

Phase one

SUB HEADING

Anti-pesto launch system

CUTAWAY HERE

Phase two

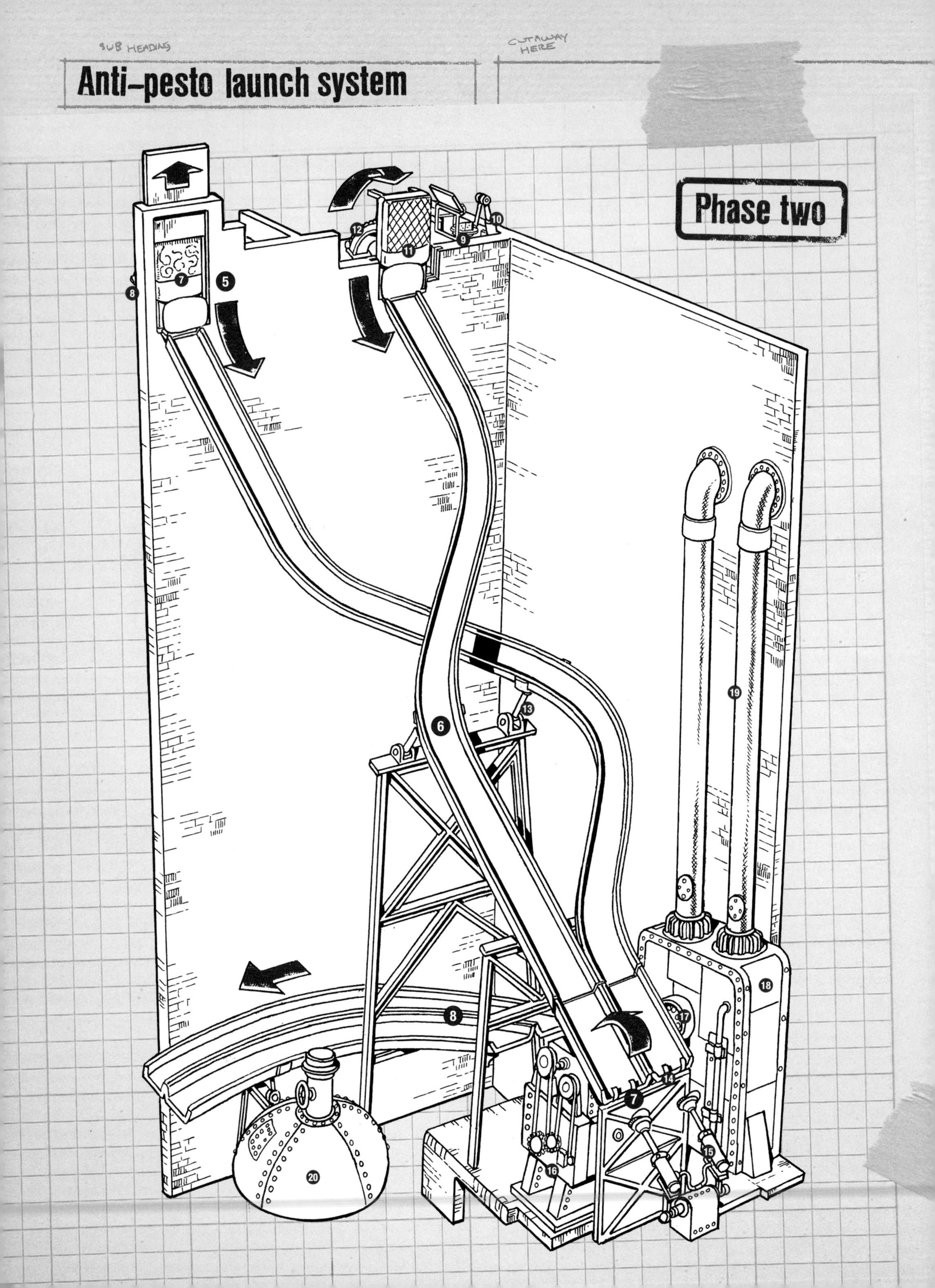

8
7
5
12
11
9
10
6
13
19
18
8
17
14
7
15
16
20

Phase three

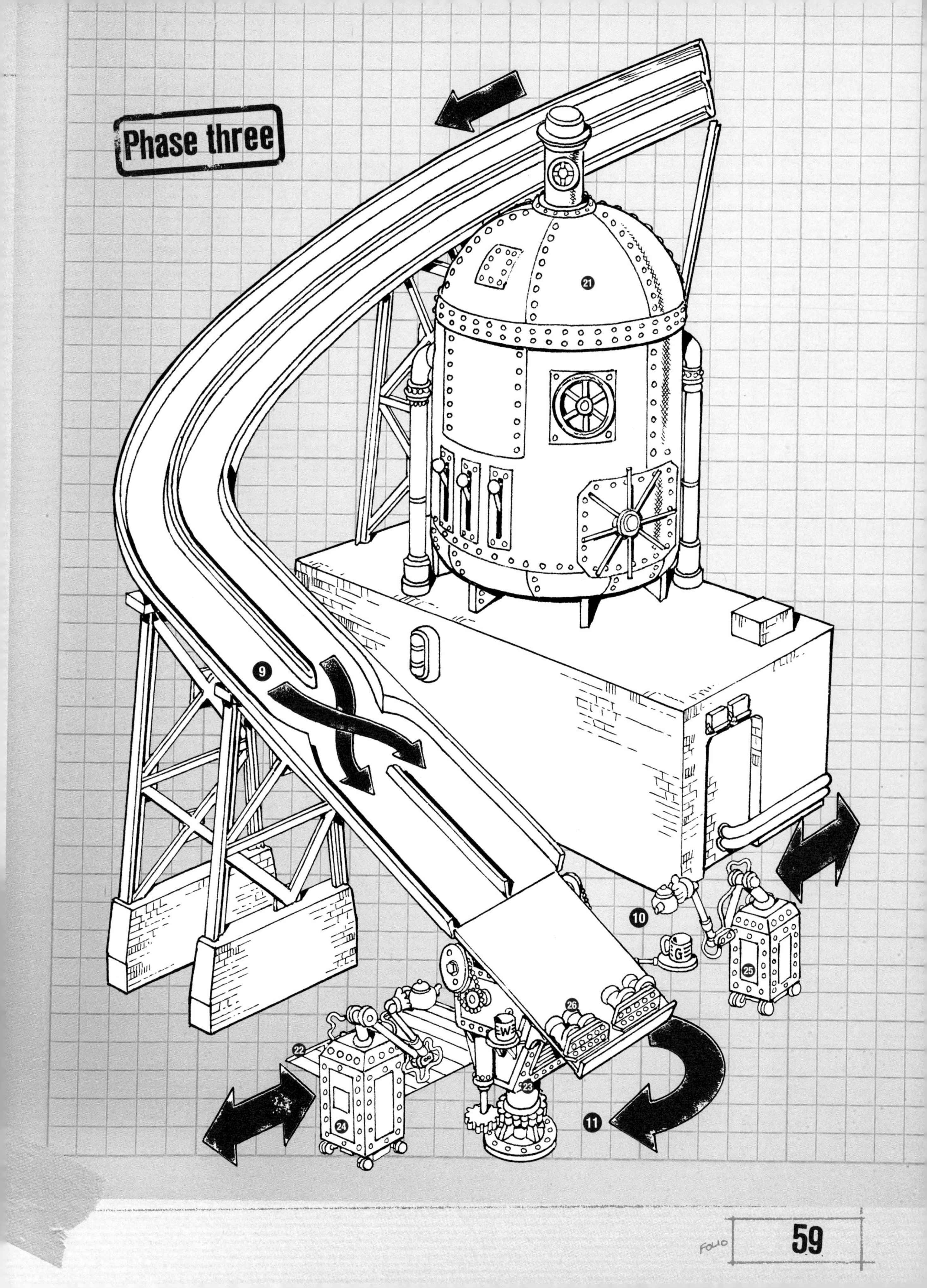
21
9
10
G
25
26
W
22
23
24
11

Phase four

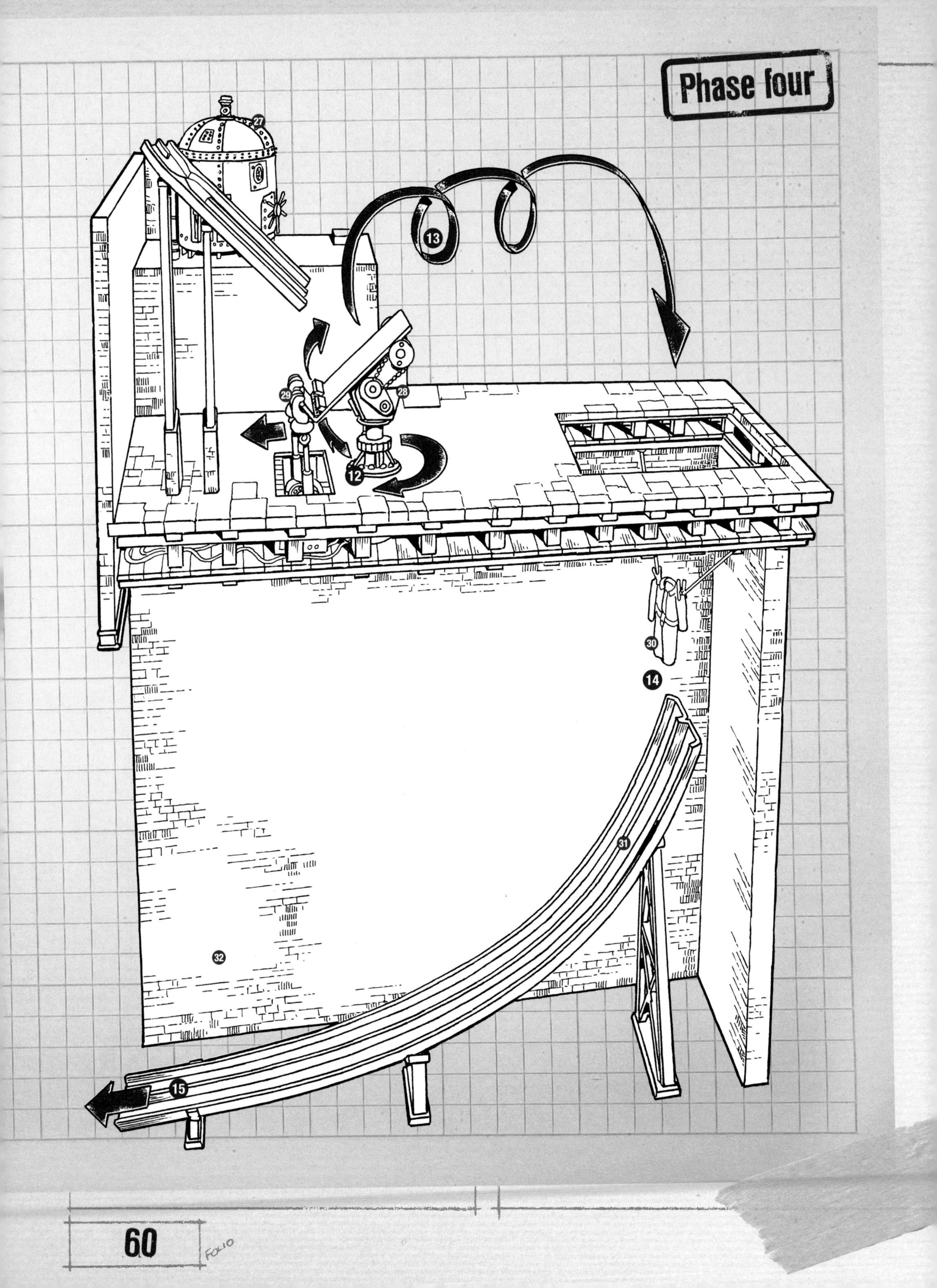
27
13
29
28
12
30
14
31
32
15

Phase five

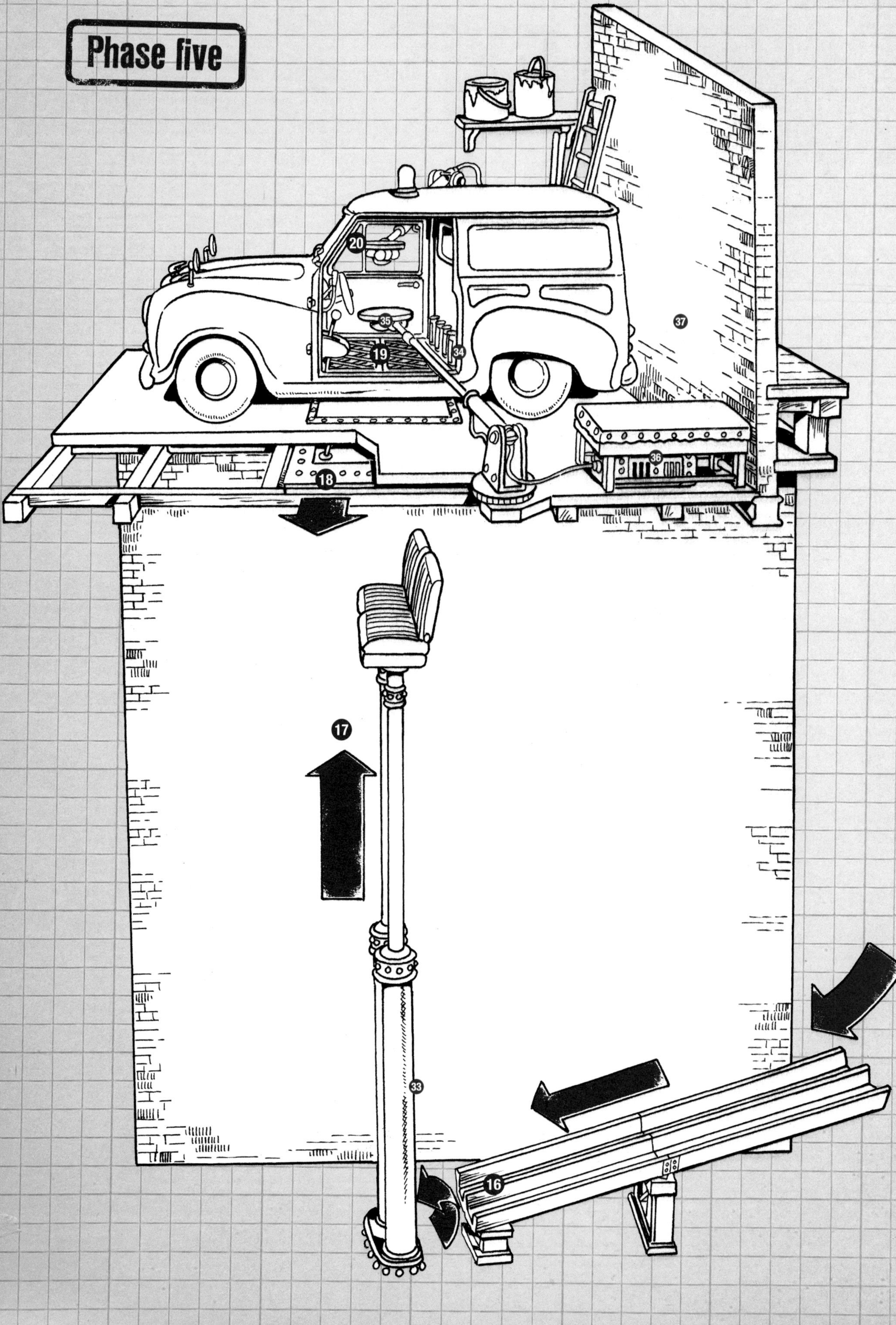
20
35
19
34
37
18
36
17
33
16

MAIN HEADING

GARDEN EXIT SYSTEM

SUB HEADING

Contents

CONTENTS LIST

PAGE NO.

SUB HEADING

General description

BODY COPY

DROP CAP

Wallace and Gromit's various enterprises have often required the use of a vehicle, most notably either the motorbike and sidecar or the Austin A35 Van. On many occasions, a quick getaway is called for, whether to dash to an urgent window-cleaning assignment, respond to a pest-control emergency, or make the early-morning bread delivery run. Time is of the essence, and Wallace and Gromit have devised many elaborate contraptions to get them from the house, into their vehicle and ready to go in the shortest time possible. It is essential therefore that not a moment is lost as the vehicle finally leaves the garage.

Upon exiting the garage the vehicle passes over a discreet pressure pad, which is built into, and disguised as part of, the garden path. The load pushes down on a pressure switch beneath, which activates several mechanisms hidden below the ground. The first is the garden pond plinth, which is rotated through 180 degrees to reveal a continuation of the driveway on the underside. The plinth rotates on a hardened steel axle, the movement being actuated by a high-torque electric motor and transfer pulley and gears.

Having passed over the pond, all that now lies between the van and the road is the garden wall and fence. A complex system of ropes, pulleys, flywheels and counterweights, driven by further electric motors and servomechanisms contained in a single housing, act to lower the garden wall into the ground (leaving the coping stones flush with the path) and raise the fence out of the way, allowing the van to pass. The mechanism to raise the fence panel is contained within one of the garden wall columns and actuated from beneath.

The entire 'basement' below the garden path is accessible via a door from the cellar of the house, enabling maintenance work to be carried out as required.

Once the van has cleared the garden wall, the mechanisms are reversed, and the garden returns to normal.

MAIN PICTURE

FOLIO

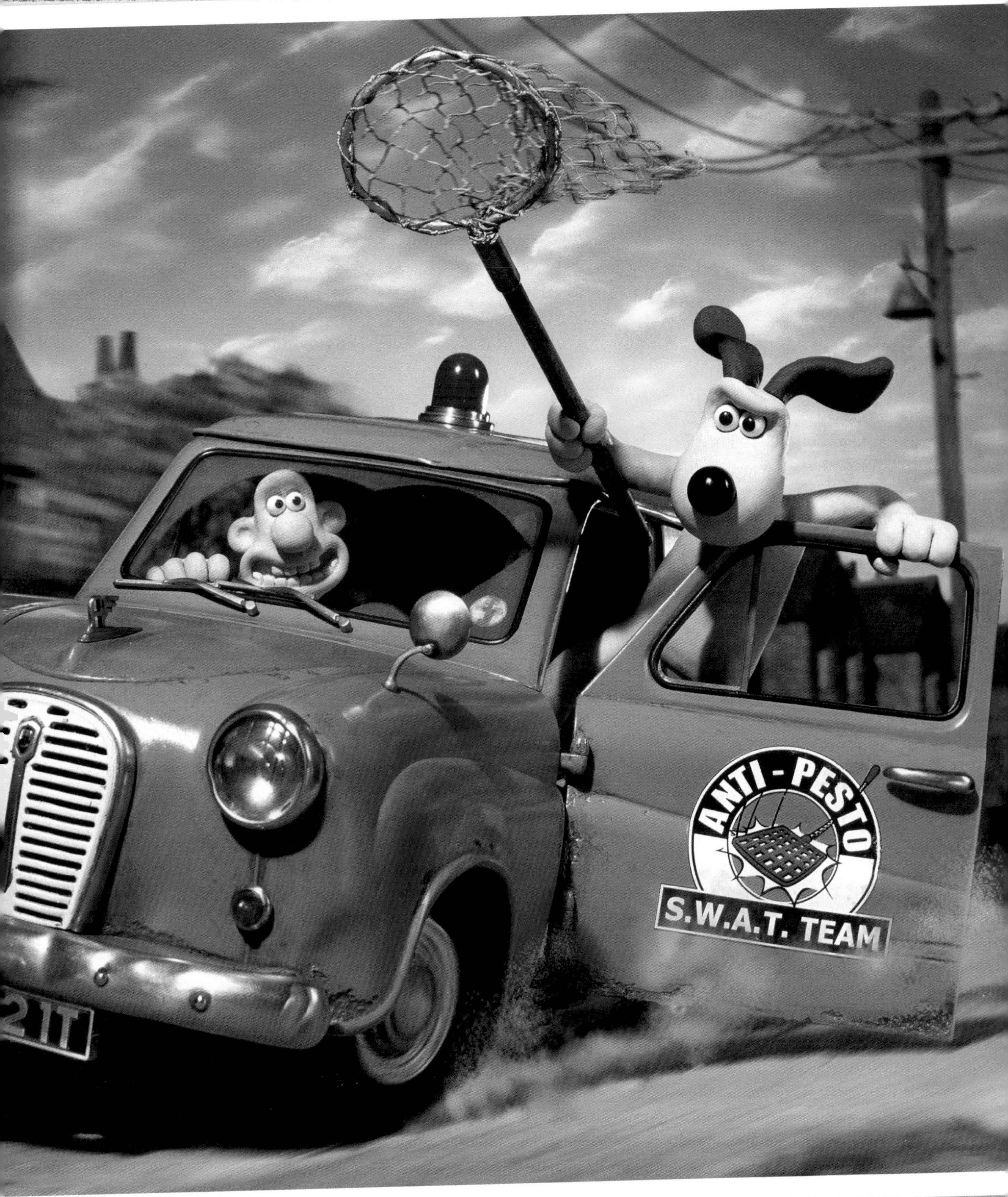
ANTI-PESTO
S.W.A.T. TEAM

SUB HEADING

CUTAWAY HERE

Garden Exit System

BULLET LIST

❶ Garden gadget activation pressure pad. As the van drives towards the pond, the paving lowers slightly and activates a pressure switch controlling the pond, wall and fence mechanisms.

❷ Pressure switch.

❸ Control box.

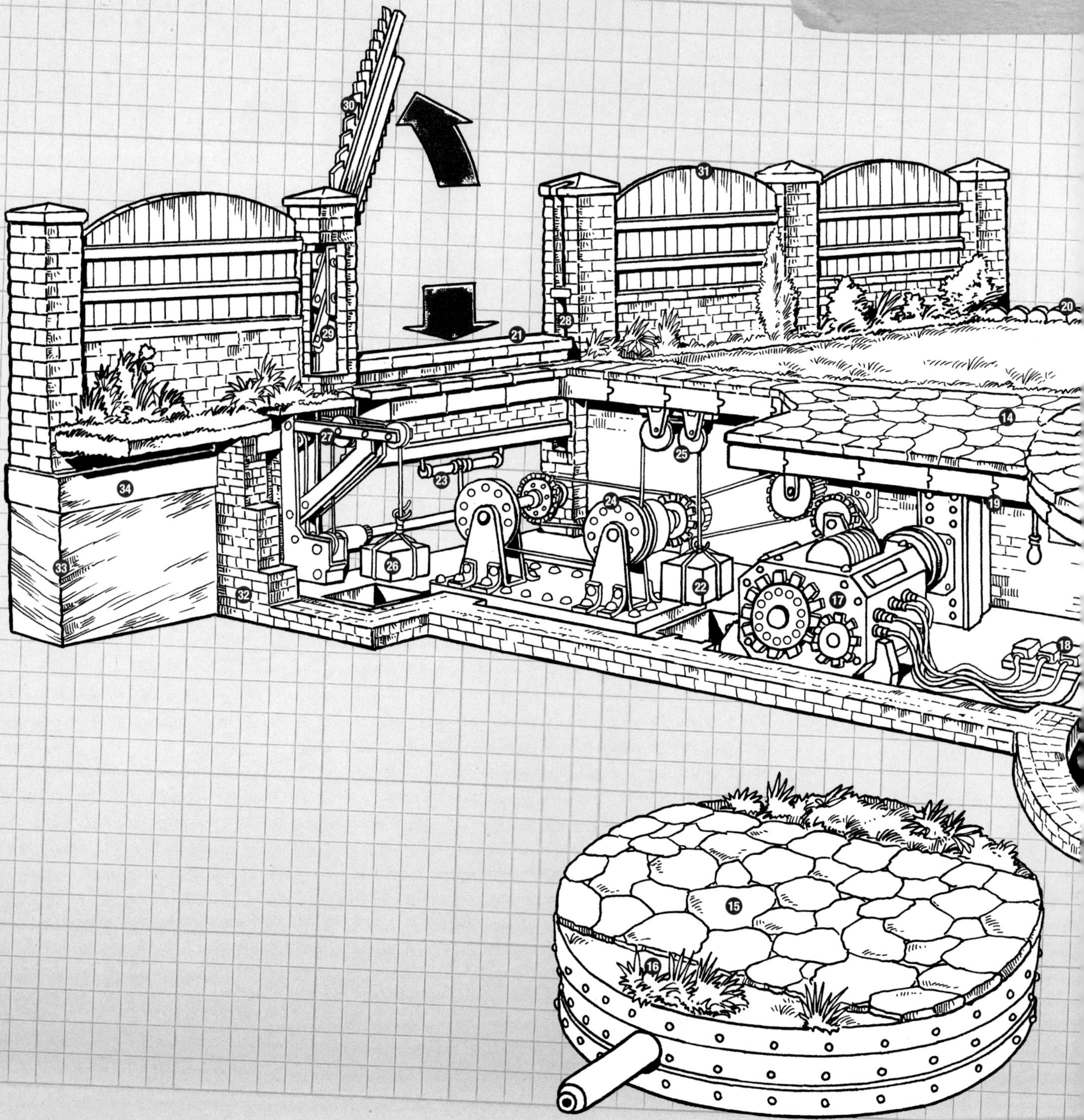
30
31
29
21
28
20
27
25
14
23
34
24
19
26
22
33
32
17
18
15
16

FOLIO

4 Door to basement from garage and cellar.

5 Well-kept lawn.

6 Steel-bonded plinth rotates to reveal a continuation of the driveway on the underside, immediately before the van passes over it.

7 The gnome's fishing rod is connected to the plinth and rotates with it.

8 Pond statue.

9 Top side of 'pond' is covered in clear resin, creating a water-like effect.

10 Garden gnome sitting on the pond's paved surround maintains its position as the plinth rotates.

11 Hardened-steel pond rotation axle.

12 Plinth rotation gearing.

13 Plinth rotation clearance pit.

14 Crazy-paving driveway.

15 Underside of plinth is designed to match the crazy paving of the driveway leading from the garage to the disguised garden wall exit.

16 Artificial plants.

17 Electric motors.

18 Power distribution board.

19 Interlocking concrete driveway base supports.

20 Edge of garden footpath.

21 Wall lowers to ground level allowing van to drive through.

22 Wall-lowering counterweight.

23 Wall underside lowering hook.

24 Flywheel system simultaneously controls fence raising and wall-lowering mechanisms.

25 Counterweight flywheel pulley system.

26 Fence-raising counterweight.

27 Fence-raising mechanism.

28 Fence wall slots.

29 Hollow garden wall column houses fence beam mechanism.

30 Wooden fence is raised at the same time as the wall is lowered.

31 Wall and fence facing onto West Wallaby Street.

32 Brick retaining wall of basement.

33 Subsoil.

34 Base of garden wall.

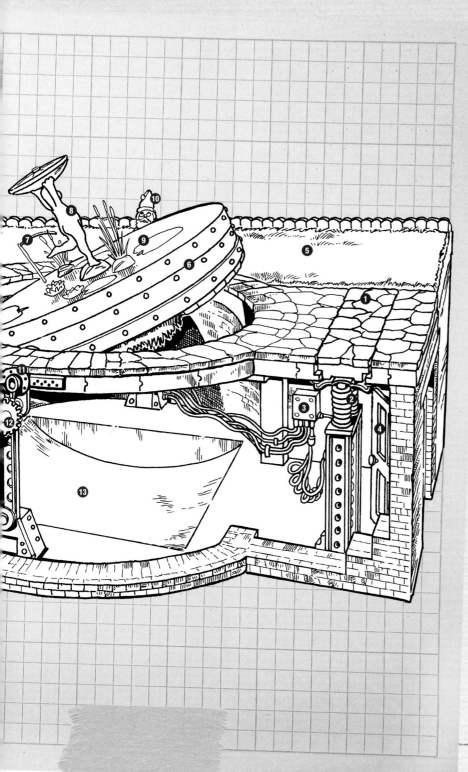

BUN VAC 6000

SUB HEADING

Contents

CONTENTS LIST   PAGE NO.

SUB HEADING

General description

BODY COPY

DROP CAP

Anti-Pesto has developed the very latest in humane pest-control technology, and the Bun Vac 6000 is the ultimate solution when it comes to large-scale rabbit infestations.

Although a large and complex device when in use, the Bun Vac 6000 compacts neatly into a 'pod', which replaces the rear section of the Austin A35 Van. While in transit the pod makes the Anti-Pesto van appear completely normal from the outside. Upon arrival at the scene of the rabbit infestation, Bun Vac deployment is initiated by a button in the cab.

First, hydraulic support legs are extended from each side of the vehicle to provide stability when the Bun Vac is in use. The sides and back of the 'pod' fold down in three sections, after which they are completely removed by hand. This reveals the Bun Vac in its compact stowed state, and full deployment commences immediately as various hydraulically actuated components are extended and slotted into place to form the lower bodywork of the device.

The main section of the Bun Vac comprises upper and lower cylinders, which are formed from glass panels and supported by four stanchions positioned around the lower cylinder. The resulting structure is a large vacuum cylinder, which is airtight. The steel cylinder cap comprises a vacuum pipe attachment valve and filter, to which a series of vacuum pipes can be fitted. Finally, a control panel and operator's seat attach to the top rim of the lower cylinder

A large suction fan is fitted into the centre of the base of the cylinder. During operation, this draws air out of the cylinder, thus creating a high vacuum inside. As a result, air is sucked into the top of the cylinder through the valve inlet and the various vacuum pipes. The last pipe ends with the 'bunny retrieval attachment' and this is placed over a convenient rabbit hole in the ground, thus extending the suction of the vacuum throughout the entire warren.

Rabbits are sucked up the vacuum pipe and deposited in the glass cylinder where they remain safely trapped but completely unharmed before being removed via an airtight retrieval hatch in the lower cylinder.

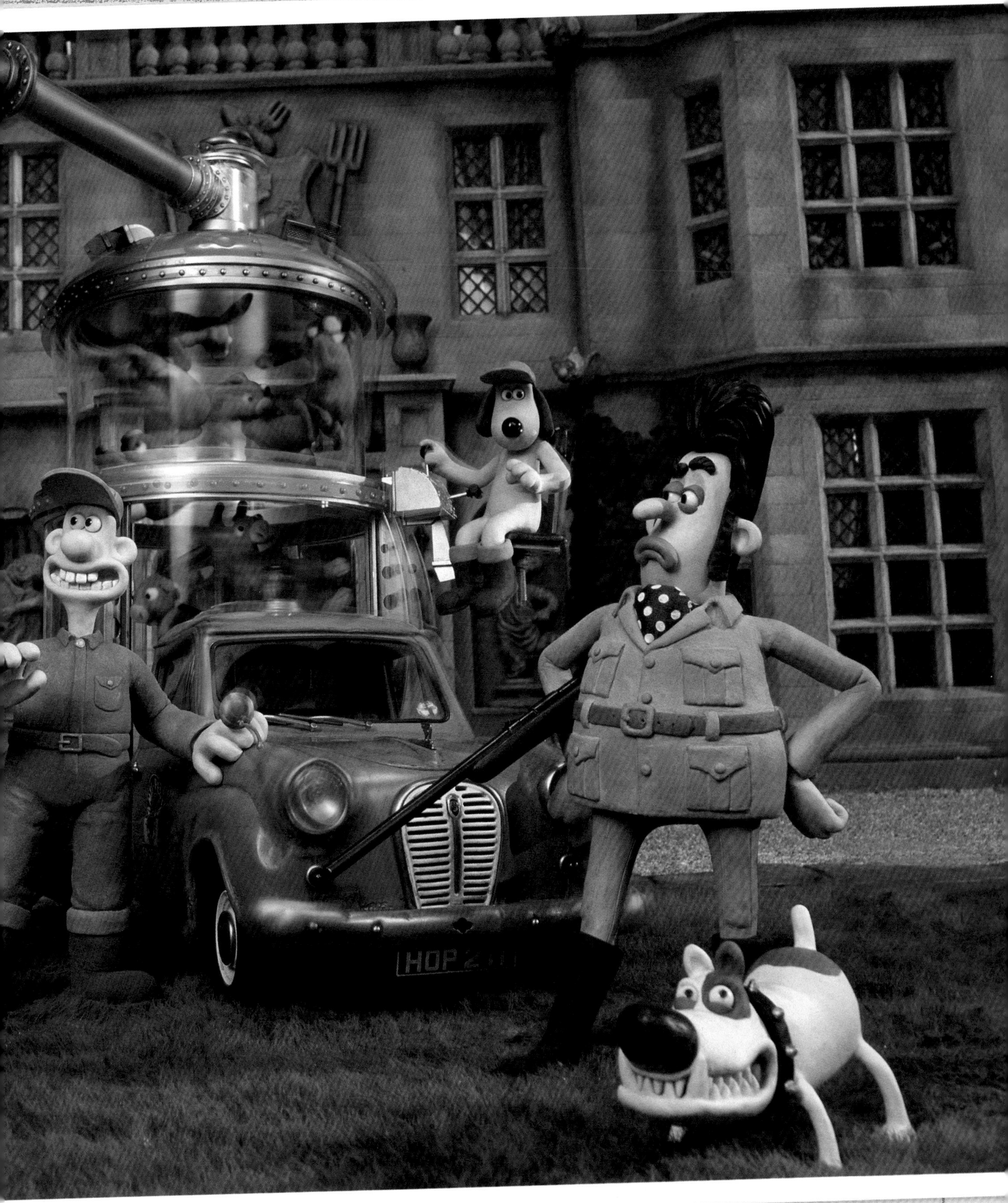

SUB HEADING

CUTAWAY HERE

Bun Vac 6000 (deployment)

BULLET LIST

1. Wing mirror.
2. Gear lever.
3. Speedometer.
4. Van de-ice, de-mist and de-mud control panel.
5. Bun Vac 6000 activation button.
6. Hydraulic vehicle support leg (deployed when Bun Vac is in use).
7. Chassis reinforcement panel for support leg.
8. Four lower cylinder glass panels deploy outwards and around to form an airtight seal as upper cylinder is raised.
9. Hydraulic arm lifts upper cylinder into position (retracts before lower cylinder panels slide into place).
10. One of four lower cylinder support stanchions making an airtight seal when in fully deployed position.
11. Upper cylinder glass panel.
12. Passenger side rear van wall and roof deployed (before manual detachment).
13. Driver's side rear van panel and roof deployed (before manual detachment).
14. Bun Vac lower bodywork stowed horizontally in segments beneath lower cylinder filter and deployed into vertical position to form an airtight skirt.
15. Bun Vac lower bodywork deployment ram.
16. Stowed vehicle support leg.
17. Heat ventilation grille in stowed position.
18. Heat ventilation grille in deployed position.
19. Each cooling fan tips forward and drops into adjacent slots in the Bun Vac's lower bodywork.
20. Cooling fan positioning slots.
21. Suction fan drive chain.
22. Suction fan reversible gearing.
23. Lower cylinder segment positioning ram.
24. Suction fan.
25. Position-adjustable lower cylinder filter.
26. Cooling fan in stowed position.
27. Rear light wiring.
28. Electric motor.
29. Upper cylinder filter.
30. Adjustable valve airtight inner tube.
31. Attachment valve height adjustment gear (valve stowed inside upper cylinder for transit).
32. Attachment valve pressure control handle.
33. Vacuum pipe attachment valve in raised position.
34. Vacuum pipes stowed each side of the cylinder and attached manually.
35. Vacuum pipe observation window.
36. Bunny retrieval attachment.
37. Bun Vac control panel mounts onto rim of lower cylinder.
38. Padded operator's seat.
39. Control panel attachment bolts.
40. Control panel wiring.
41. Safety warning light.

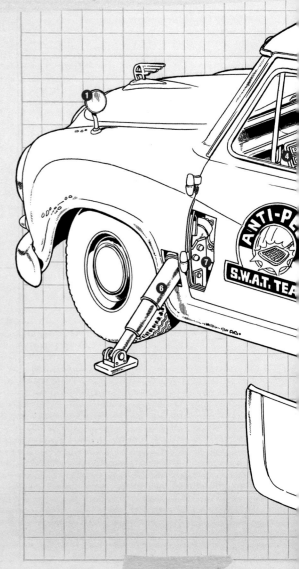

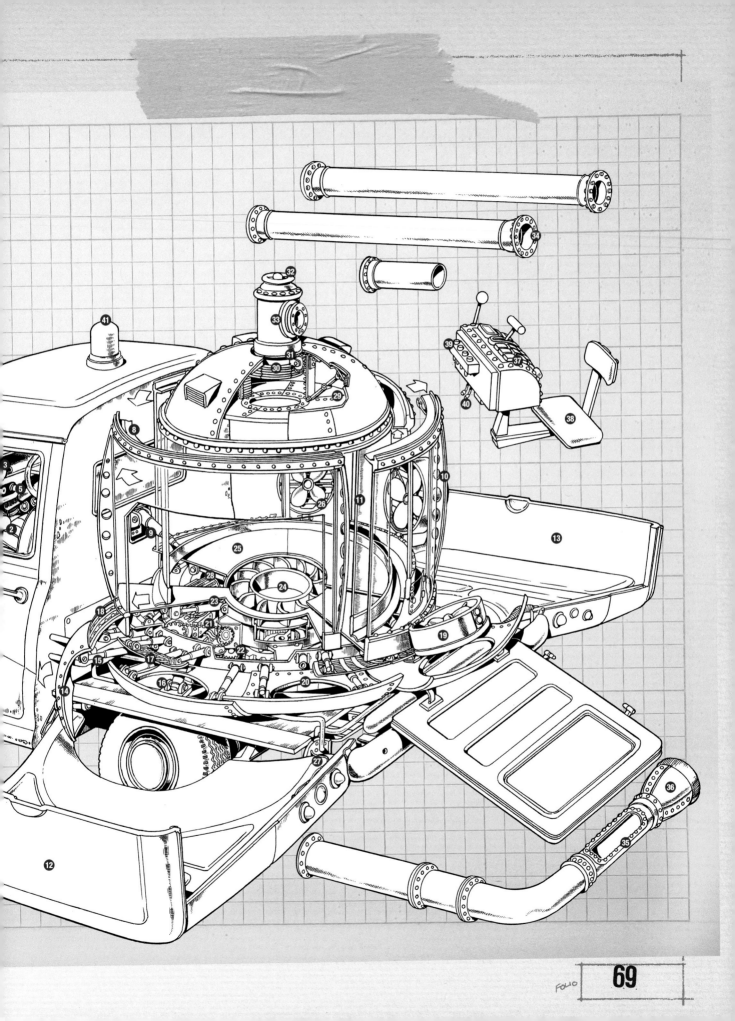

SUB HEADING

CUTAWAY HERE

Bun Vac 6000 (fully deployed)

BULLET LIST

1. Bunny retrieval attachment.
2. Ground seal.
3. Vacuum pipe contents observation window.
4. Vacuum pipes in manually deployed position.
5. Bun Vac control panel.
6. Control panel operator's seat.
7. Upper vacuum cylinder in raised position.
8. Airtight seals and lower cylinder support stanchions.
9. Airtight rabbit retrieval hatch.
10. Heat ventilation grille.
11. Cooling fans.
12. Hydraulic vehicle support leg.

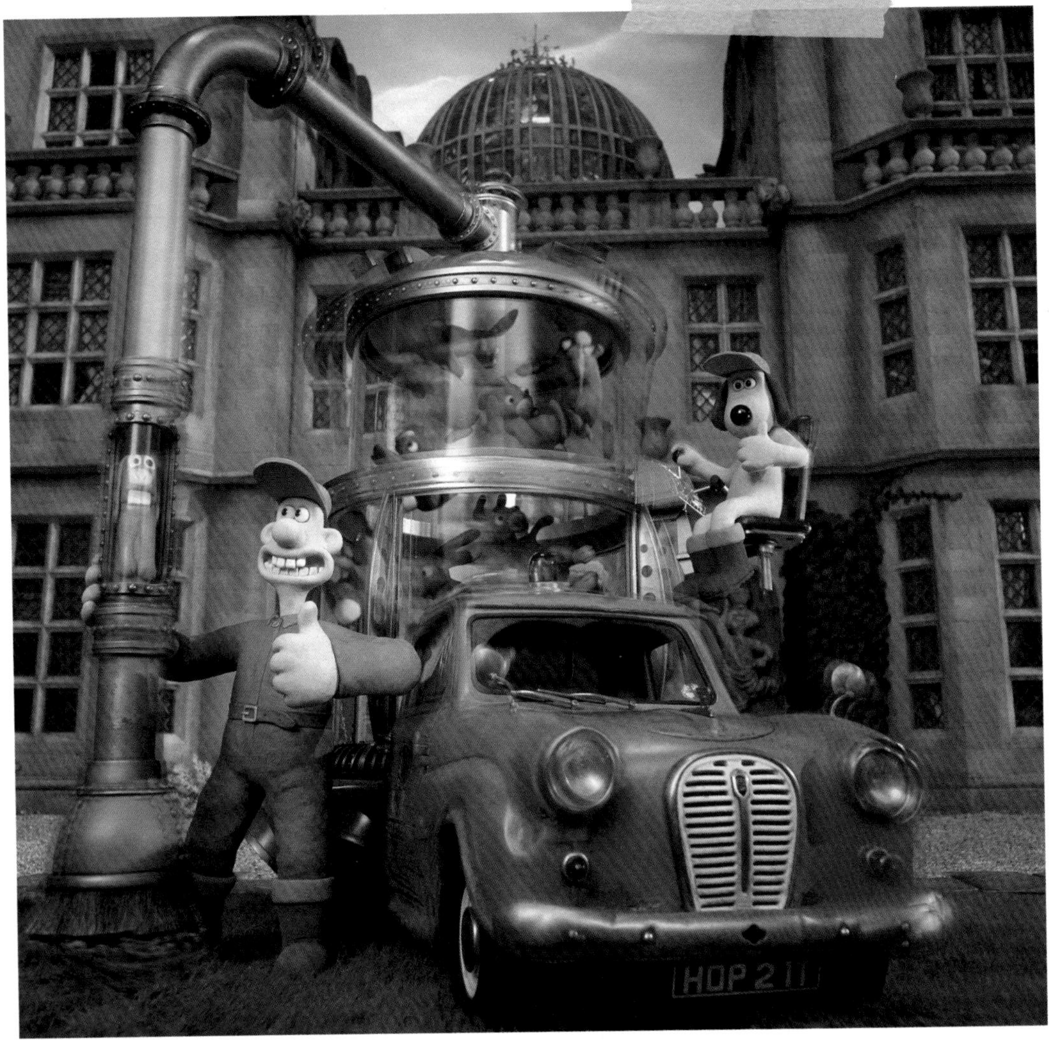
HOP 211

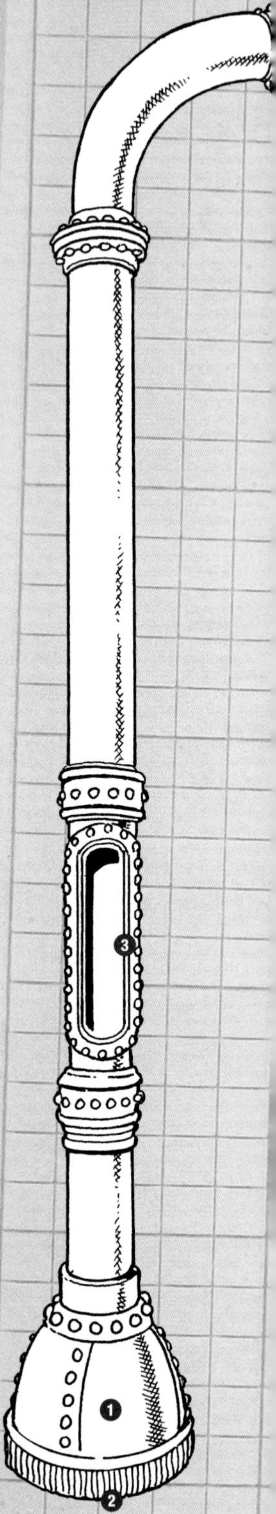
3
1
2

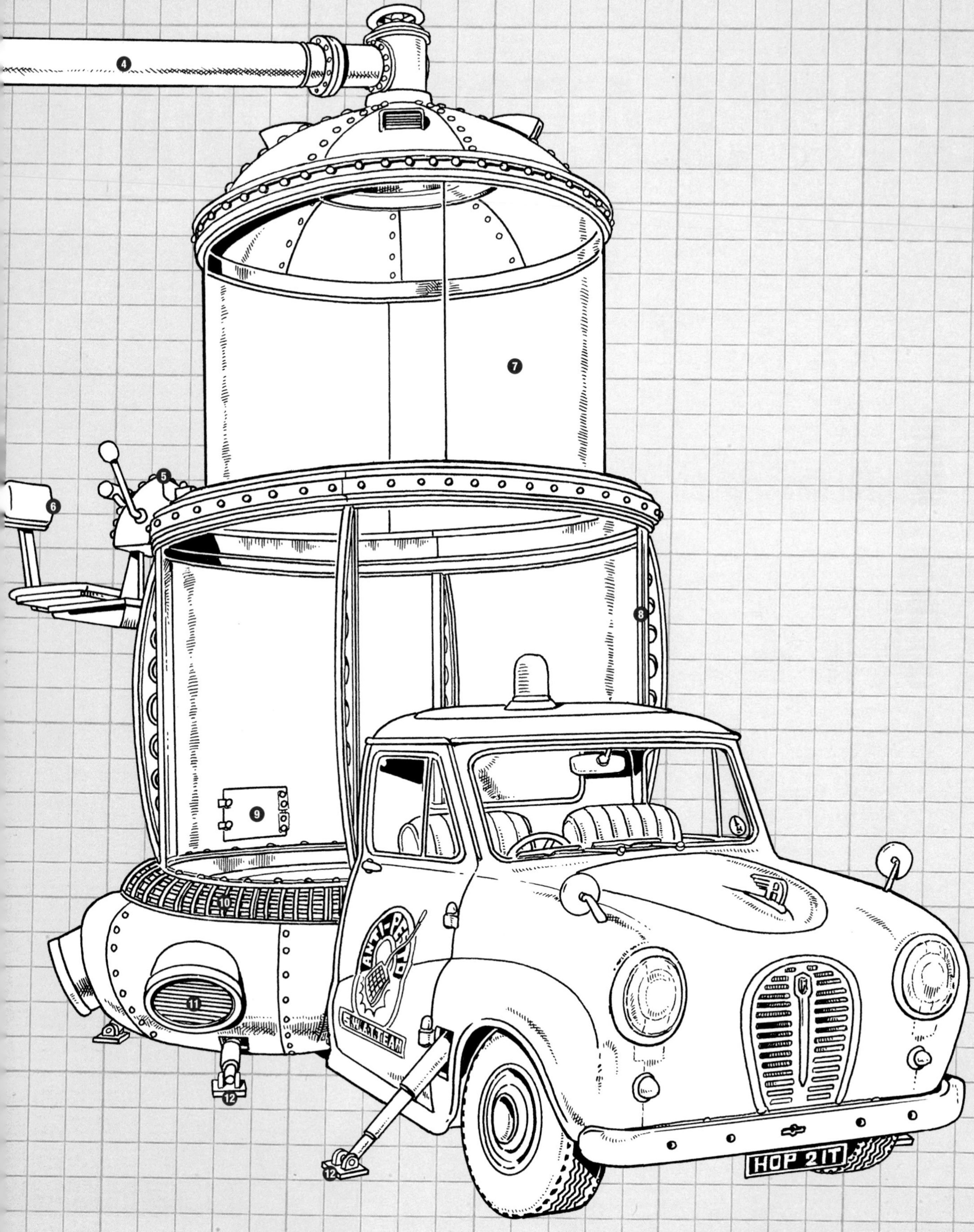

4
5
6
7
8
9
10
11
12
12
S.W.A.T.TEAM
HOP 2IT

MAIN HEADING

MIND MANIPULATION-O-MATIC

MAIN PICTURE

SUB HEADING

Contents

CONTENTS LIST

PAGE N

SUB HEADING

General description

BODY COPY

DROP CAP

While most of Wallace's inventions are designed as time- and labour-saving devices, occasionally one comes along with a far more subtle and sophisticated purpose. One such invention is the Mind Manipulation-O-Matic, which is a machine for the removal of unwanted thoughts and desires.

The main part of the Mind Manipulation-O-Matic comprises a glass thought-collection dome mounted on a pair of cantilevered positioning arms. This apparatus is stored in a cabinet in Wallace's bedroom and deployed through hatches in the floor of the bedroom and the ceiling of the dining room below. Horizontal positioning is accomplished by the aforementioned cantilevered arms while vertical positioning is achieved by a telescopic section and flexible conduit. The thought-collection dome is anatomically shaped and fitted with an adjustable forehead clamp. During use, thoughts are collected by two sensor probes and signalled by an indicator bulb on each probe.

This first prototype is activated by a discreet condiment switch (pepper pot), located on the dining room table, which opens a place-mat panel to reveal a control console, which rises up from beneath the table top. From here, the main apparatus can be deployed, programmed and controlled completely. Wallace tries this first prototype out to help him lose weight using the power of the mind, but with limited success.

A second prototype is built into the cellar of 62 West Wallaby Street. Featuring a more permanent structure, this lacks the deployment and positioning apparatus of the dining-room version but features a pair of moonshine lunar panels, which provide additional power during the thought transference process. An armchair, with integrated control console and handy magazine rack, are provided for the user's comfort during extended thought-control sessions.

With a large number of recently captured rabbits to relocate, Wallace wonders if the Mind Manipulation-O-Matic can be used to clear their minds of all vegetable desires. He hastily connects his new invention to the suction pipe of the Bun Vac 6000 and attempts to brainwash the bunnies, but a malfunction results in a 'mind-meld' between Wallace and one of the rabbits, which brings unforeseen consequences.

FOLIO

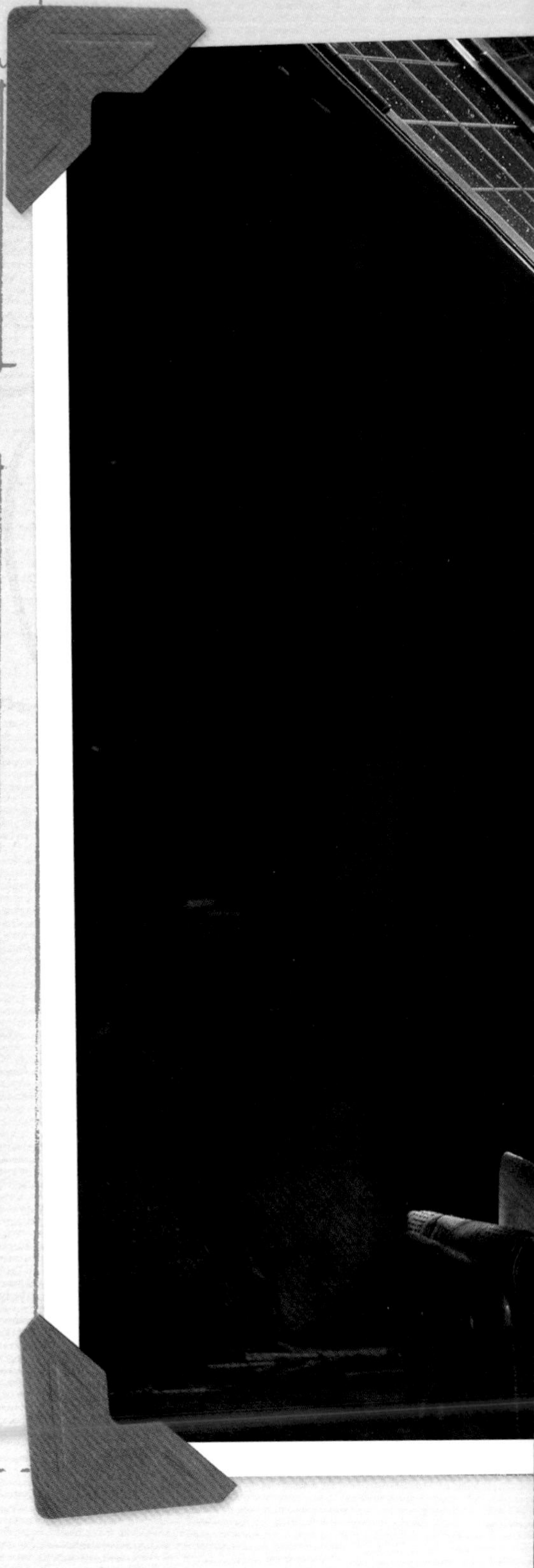

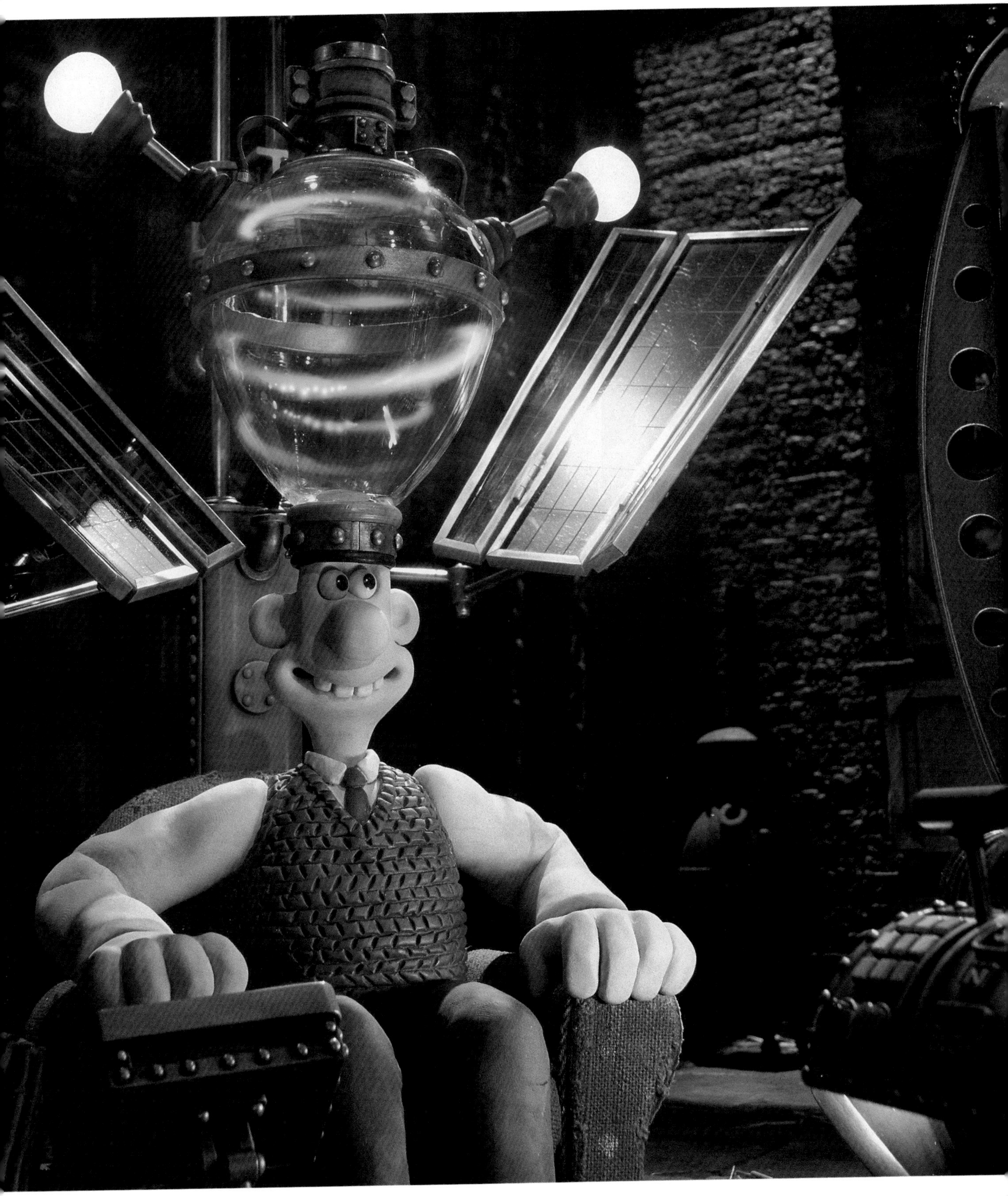

(dining room version)
Mind Manipulation–O–Matic

1. Fork.
2. Knife.
3. Salt cellar.
4. Control console activation condiment switch (pepper).
5. Control console deployment mechanism.
6. Place mat in lowered position.
7. Mind Manipulation-O-Matic control console in raised position.
8. Dining room table and tablecloth.
9. Nest of tables.
10. Decorative doily.
11. Aspidistra.
12. Padded high-impact dining room chair seat.
13. Unwanted thought and desire collection sphere.
14. Collection sphere special glass blown by Jones the Glass.
15. Thought collection sensors.
16. Retractable longlife thought extraction indicator bulbs.
17. Height adjustment grips in deployed position.
18. Height adjustment cords.
19. Mind Manipulation-O-Matic vertical deployment motor.
20. Upper cantilevered positioning arm.
21. Lower cantilevered positioning arm.
22. Sliding ceiling hatch.
23. Hatch cord winch electric motor.
24. Mind Manipulation-O-Matic horizontal deployment motor.
25. Electronics and control box.
26. Mind Manipulation-O-Matic storage cabinet in Wallace's bedroom.
27. Floor hatch pulley and cord.
28. Floor hatch.
29. Ceiling joists.
30. Ceiling hatch pulley and cord.
31. Dining room ceiling.
32. Floor hatch winch wheel.

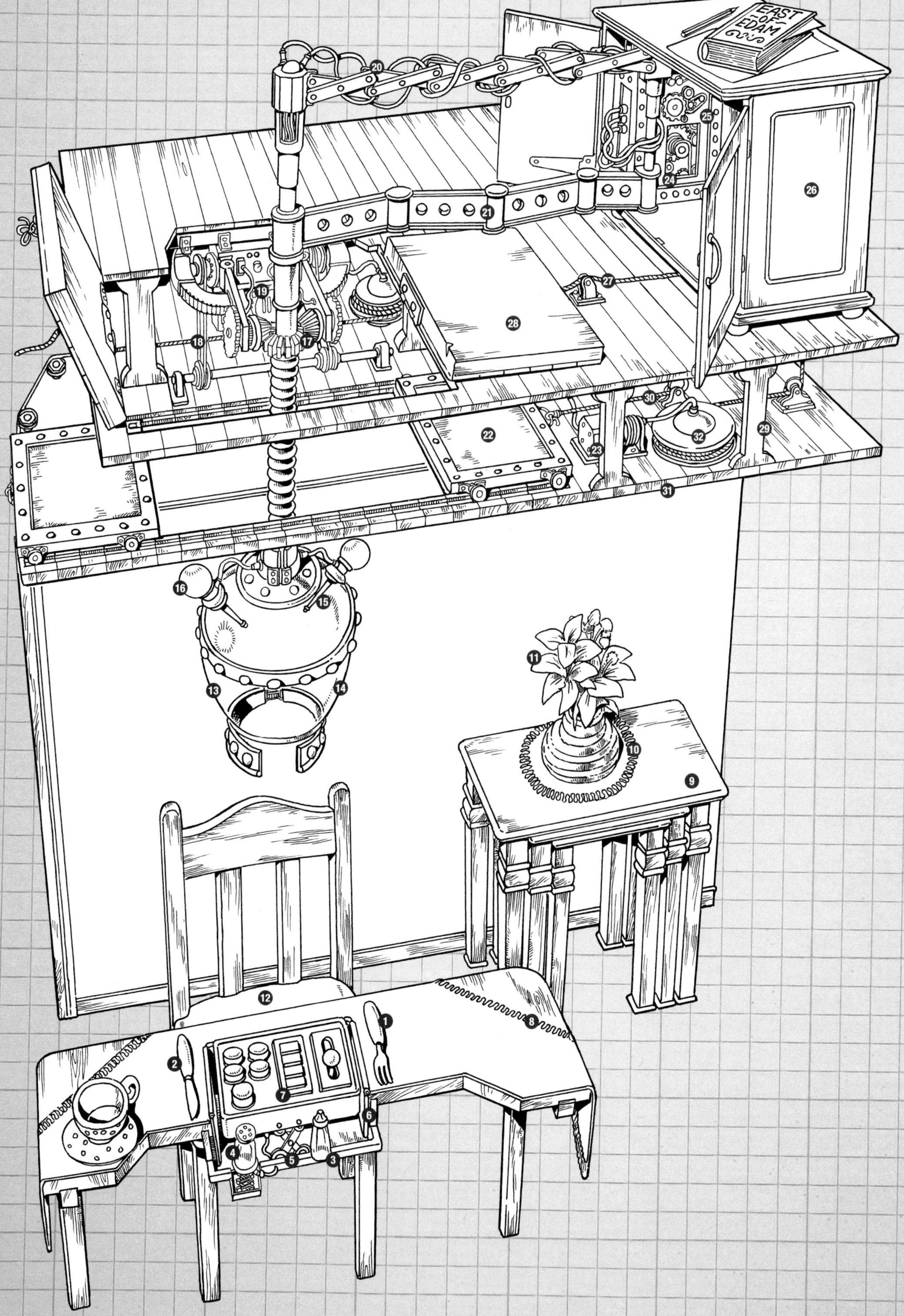

EAST
OF
EDAM
1
2
3
4
5
6
7
8
9
10
11
12
13
14
15
16
17
18
19
20
21
22
23
24
25
26
27
28
29
30
31
32

Mind Manipulation-0-Matic
(cellar version)

1. Blow 'n' suck control lever.
2. Relocated Bun Vac control panel.
3. Extended cabling for relocated control panel.
4. Toolbox, used to relocate control panel and provide a seat for the operator.
5. Electric motor.
6. Drive chain.
7. Suction fan control gearing.
8. Bodywork positioning ram.
9. Positioning ram control box.
10. Cooling fan.
11. Heat ventilation grille.
12. Suction fan.
13. Rabbit retrieval hatch.
14. Lower cylinder support stanchion.
15. Airtight rim seal.
16. Upper cylinder in raised and airtight position.
17. Upper cylinder filter.
18. Adjustable valve airtight inner tube.
19. Vacuum pipe/thought transfer tube attachment valve.
20. Attachment valve height adjustment gearing (retracted).
21. Attachment valve pressure control handle.
22. Thought transmitter and release mechanism for brainwashing.
23. Thought transfer tube.
24. Thought collection sensors.
25. Unwanted thought and desire collection sphere.
26. Longlife thought extraction indicator bulb.
27. Forehead clamp.
28. Moonshine lunar panels provide additional power to enhance mind waves during the thought transfer process.
29. Multi-angle lunar panel adjustment and support arms. Panels fold up and are stored in upright position when not in use.
30. Mind Manipulation-0-Matic support column incorporates wiring to control box behind chair.
31. Comfy chair.
32. Mind Manipulation-0-Matic control console.
33. Magazine rack.

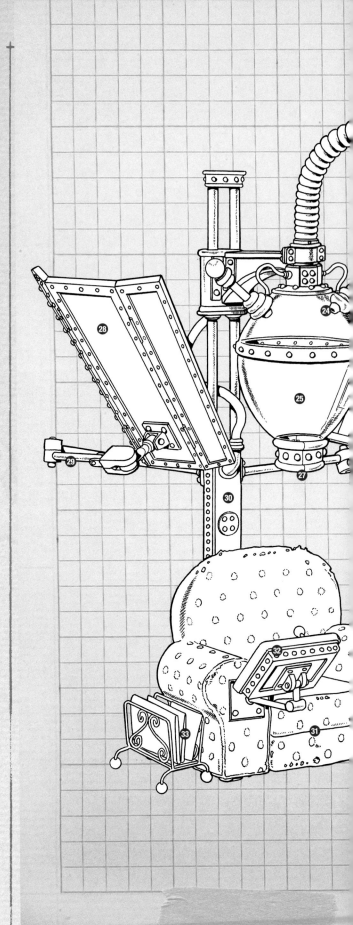

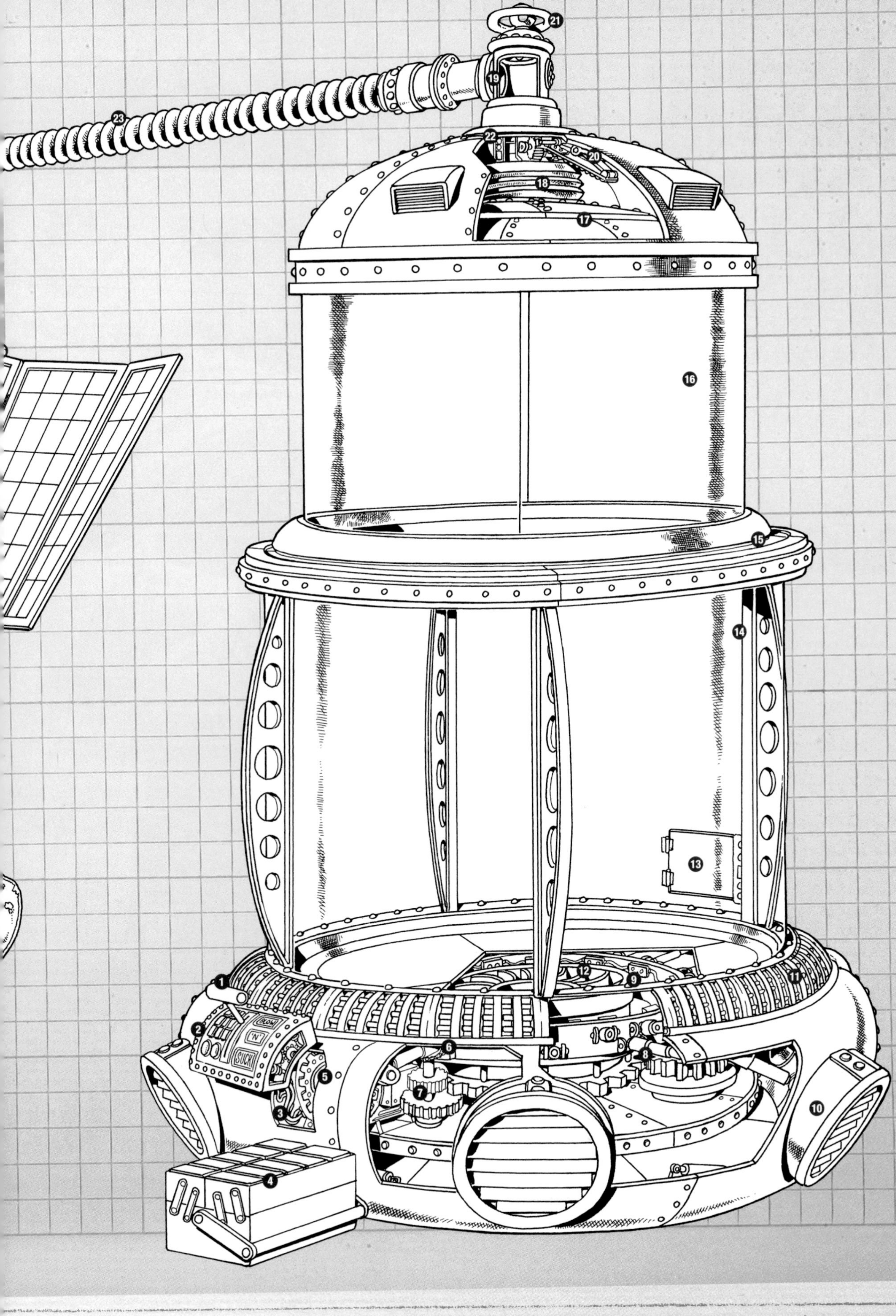
BLOW
'N'
SUCK

MAIN HEADING

AUSTIN A35 VAN

SUB HEADING

Contents

CONTENTS LIST

PAGE N

SUB HEADING

General description

BODY COPY

DROP CAP

Wallace and Gromit's faithful Austin A35 Van has undergone many modifications over the years, and here it is shown adapted for use in their Anti-Pesto pest-control business.

As a crucial part of the Anti-Pesto SWAT team rapid-response launch system, the van is fitted with access hatches below the driver and passenger seats. When open, these allow the van seats, carrying Wallace and Gromit, to pass up through hatches in the garage floor and into the cab, where they are secured automatically by self-extending support stanchions. The hatches close, and the engine Autostarter operates. This consists of a telescopic arm, which extends through the front of the engine bay, on the end of which is a mechanical hand grip and engine cranking handle.

The engine bay also houses an automatic lasso system and gearing for the special 'de-mud' mechanism, which rocks the van vigorously from side to side to shake off loose mud after callouts to fields and allotments.

The rear of the van is fitted out with a comprehensive range of pest-control equipment, including grabbers, a net, binoculars, a spade, wire cutters and a ladder.

Occasionally, certain pest problems call for special equipment, and one such example is the giant lady rabbit puppet, which Wallace and Gromit devise as a lure to catch the were-rabbit. The puppet is very large to make it visible from a distance, and very alluring in order to attract the male were-rabbit. It is mounted on the roof of the van by means of a flexible support column, which extends through the full height of the puppet. The legs and arms can be moved independently via a system of sprung linkages and control cords. The controls are operated from inside the rear of the van by Gromit who is seated on a saddle and restrained by a harness in case of tactical manoeuvres.

FOLIO

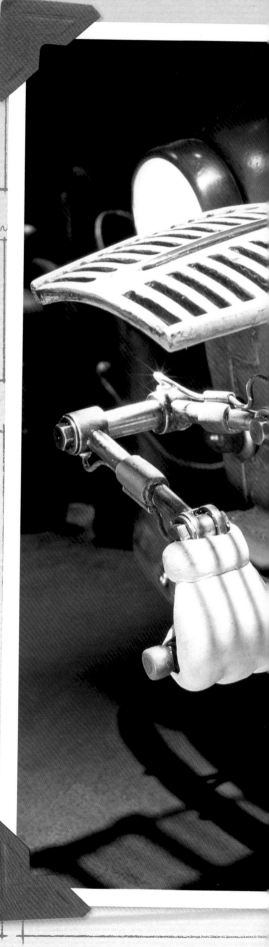

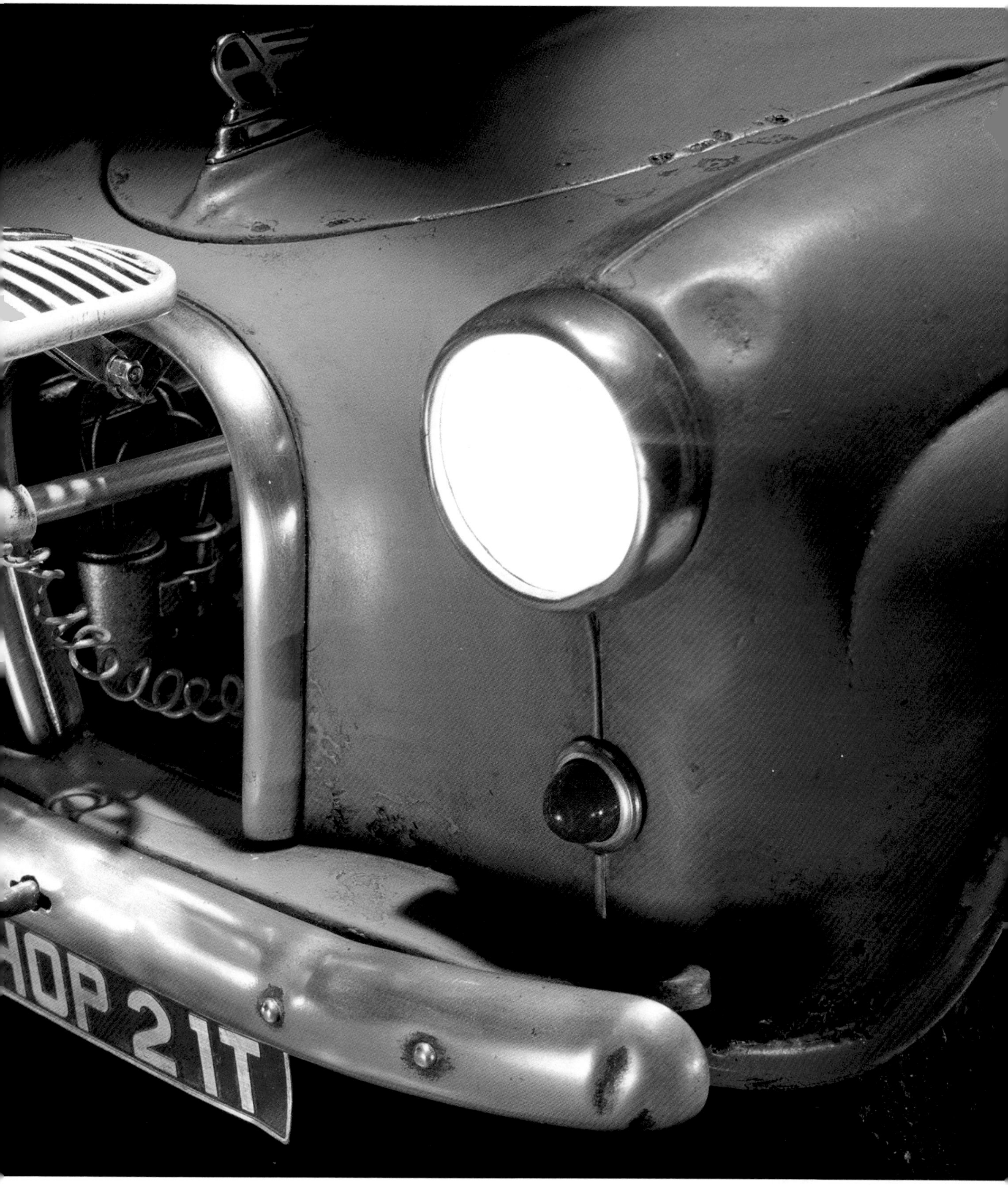
HOP 21T

Austin A35 Van

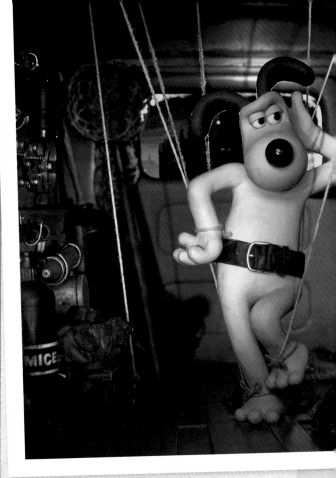

1. Multi-jointed and telescopic Autostarter control arm.
2. Radiator grille in raised position to allow Autostarter to pass through.
3. Cranking handle grip.
4. Engine cranking handle.
5. Retracted cooling fan.
6. Radiator swings back allowing Autostarter to pass through.
7. Radiator hose leading to engine.
8. Telescopic lasso rope deployment arm.
9. Lasso electric motor.
10. Lasso arm control linkage.
11. Lasso rope control and retrieval winch.
12. Austin bonnet badge swings 90 degrees and descends allowing lasso system to operate.
13. Lasso operator's control handle.
14. Steering column.
15. Battery.
16. Passenger side van support leg (retracted).
17. Mud removal control gearing (see page 74, no. 4).
18. Gear lever.
19. Passenger seat support stanchions (shown folded back to allow seat to ascend through floor access hatch (see page 61).
20. Driver's seat support stanchions shown in deployed position.
21. Floor access hatch.
22. Safety warning light.
23. Humane mice knockout gas cylinder.
24. 'Operation clean-up' bucket.
25. Shears.
26. Rabbit grabber.
27. Binoculars.
28. Hammer.
29. Sink plunger.
30. Pest-catching net.
31. End of step ladder (stowed on left side of van compartment).
32. Humane rat knockout gas cylinder.
33. Wire cutters.
34. Spade.
35. Puppet operator's control harness.

36. Puppet operator's saddle.
37. Right arm control cord.
38. Left arm control cord.
39. Right foot control cord.
40. Left foot control cord.
41. Eyebrow control pedal.
42. Flexible puppet support column.
43. High-strength puppet subframe wrapped in chicken wire.
44. Fully sprung leg movement linkage.
45. Central control column (through which eyebrow control cord is fed).
46. Heavy-duty elastic bands.
47. Chicken wire upper body.
48. Fake fur for extra rabbit authenticity.
49. Body curvature specially designed to attract the were-rabbit.
50. Bow for feminine touch.
51. Fully sprung arm movement linkage.
52. Colourful female rabbit lip gloss.
53. Plastic balls painted to resemble pearls for added allure.
54. Left winking eyebrow controlled via cord from foot pedal.

FOLIO

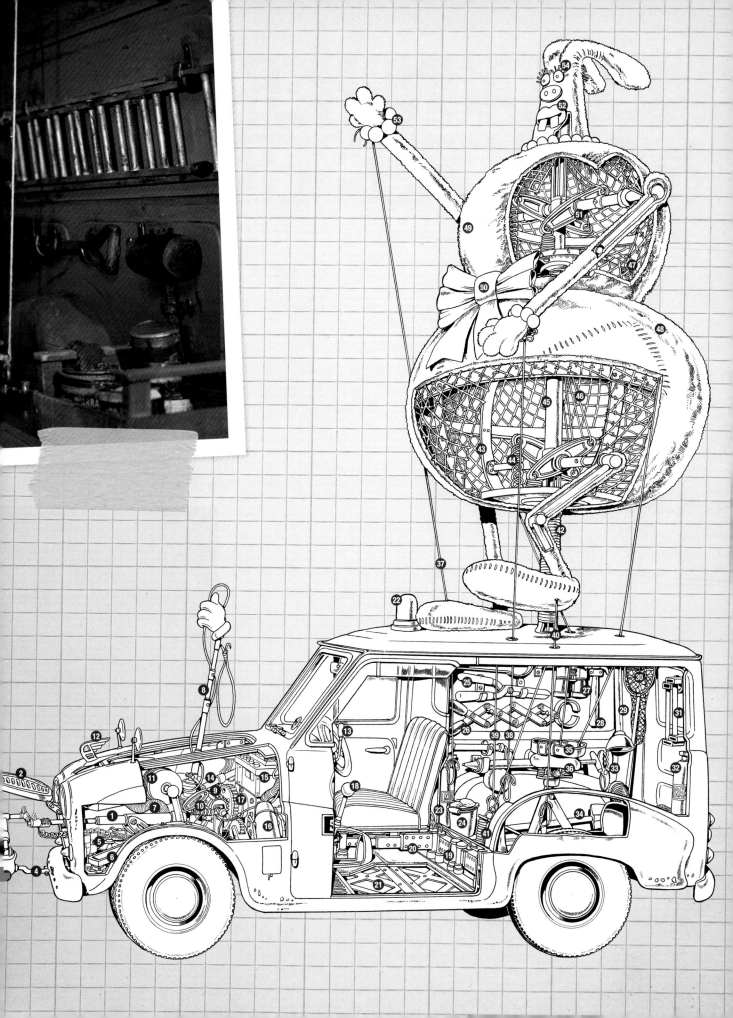

BED LAUNCHER & AUTODRESSER

Contents

General description

BODY COPY

DROP CAP

Even the most successful inventions require occasional tweaking and modification to make them better still, and two such devices are Wallace's trusty Bed Launcher and Auto Dresser.

The Bed Launcher is activated by a push-button on the bedside control panel. This starts a winch motor, located above the bedroom ceiling, which, assisted by a large counterweight, lifts the head end of the mattress causing Wallace to slide out of the foot end of the bed. At the same time, an under-floor motor winches open a two-door hatch via a system of pulleys and cords, allowing Wallace to slide neatly through to the dining room below. If Wallace should get stuck part way through the floor hatch (perhaps due to his expanding waistline) then extra assistance may be called upon. The Activated Assistance mechanism consists of a single lever, which is mounted on the wall of the dining room and operated by Gromit. This opens the doors of the wardrobe in Wallace's bedroom and releases a large softwood mallet from within. The force of the mallet 'assists' Wallace through the hatch before being automatically wound back up into the wardrobe ready for the next use.

Once safely though the hatch from the bedroom above, Wallace lands on a dining chair at the breakfast table, and the Auto Dresser system is immediately activated. Trousers are pulled over Wallace's legs by the Auto Dresser's arms, which extend forward either side of the chair, while slippers are deployed by a separate device located on the underside of the table. The Auto Dresser then pulls Wallace's tank top, complete with shirt body and tie, over his head before two ceiling-mounted articulated arms attach the shirt sleeves to complete his outfit.

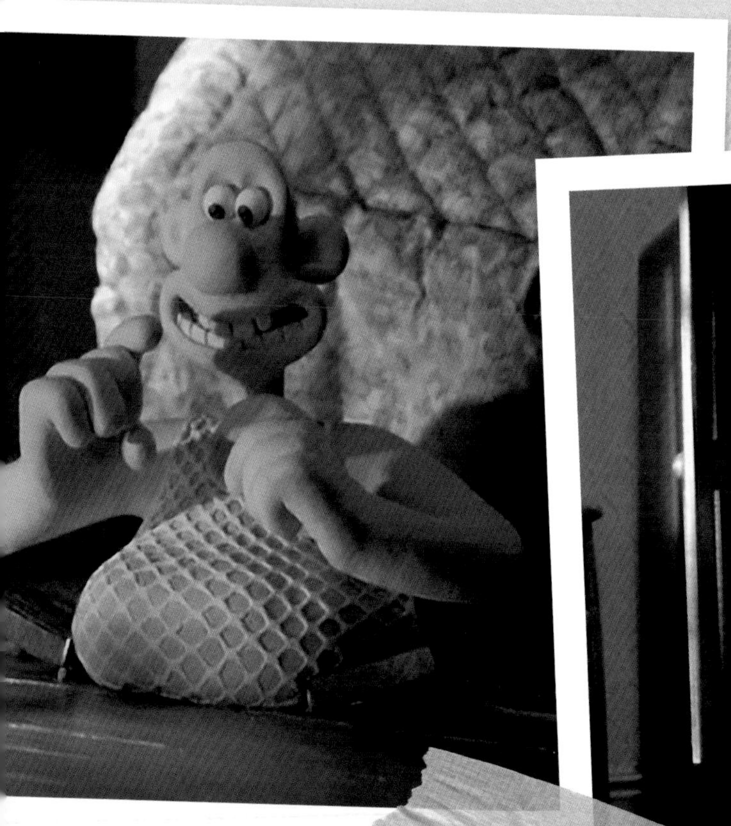
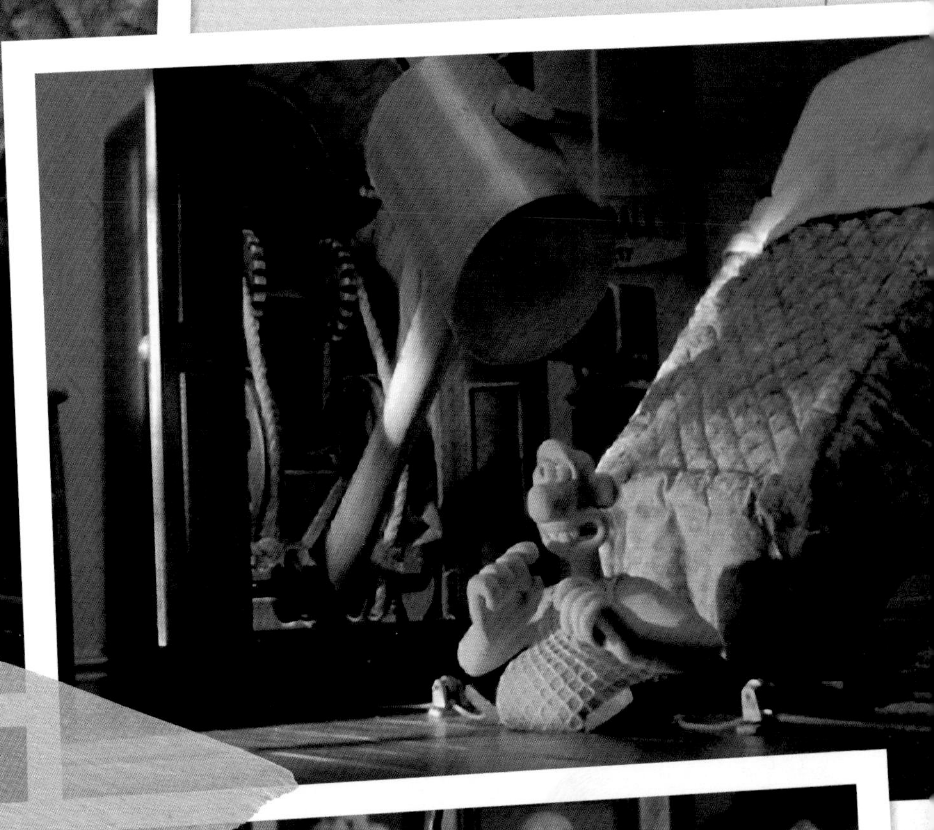
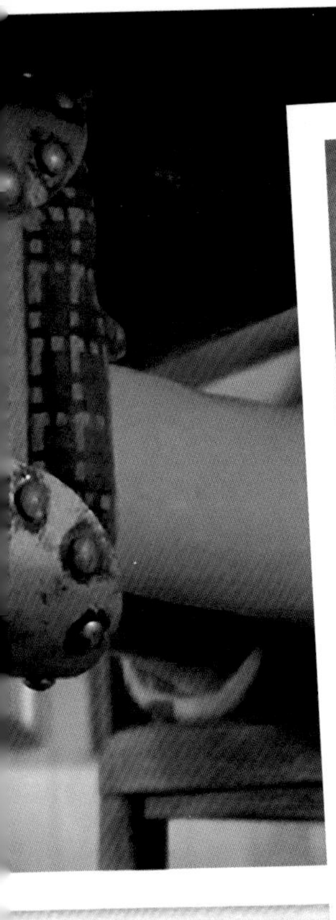
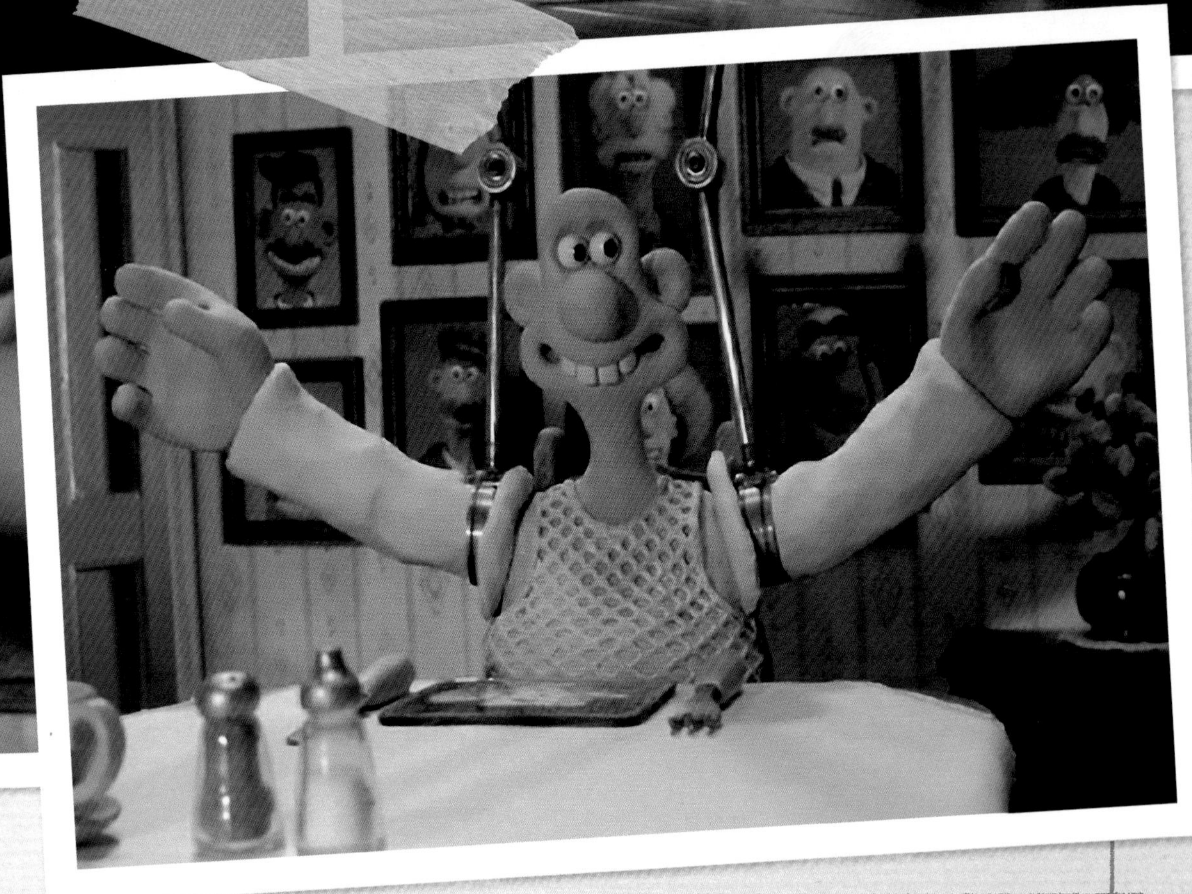

Bed Launcher (Activated Assistance version)

1. Wallace presses the launch activation button on the bedside control panel.

2. The bed tips up and Wallace slides down to the floor hatch.

3. The floor hatch doors have opened to let Wallace through.

4. If Wallace gets stuck, Gromit throws the Activated Assistance Lever (see page 86).

5. The lever activates the drop mechanism of the large mallet in the bedroom wardrobe.

❶ Bedside call system control box.

❷ Mattress lift winch motor.

❸ Mattress lift counterweight.

❹ Strengthened bed mattress.

❺ Floor hatch pulley and cord.

❻ Bedside table.

❼ Tray of cheese and crackers.

❽ Cabinet containing Mind Manipulation-O-Matic (see page 72)

❾ Hatch cord winch motor.

❿ Hatch cord winch reel.

⓫ Sliding ceiling hatch.

⓬ Ceiling joists.

⓭ Clothes rail and hanging clothes.

⓮ Side panels of wardrobe used to store clothes.

⓯ Mallet drop release mechanism.

⓰ Softwood mallet head.

⓱ Drop mechanism gearing cogs and rewind mechanism.

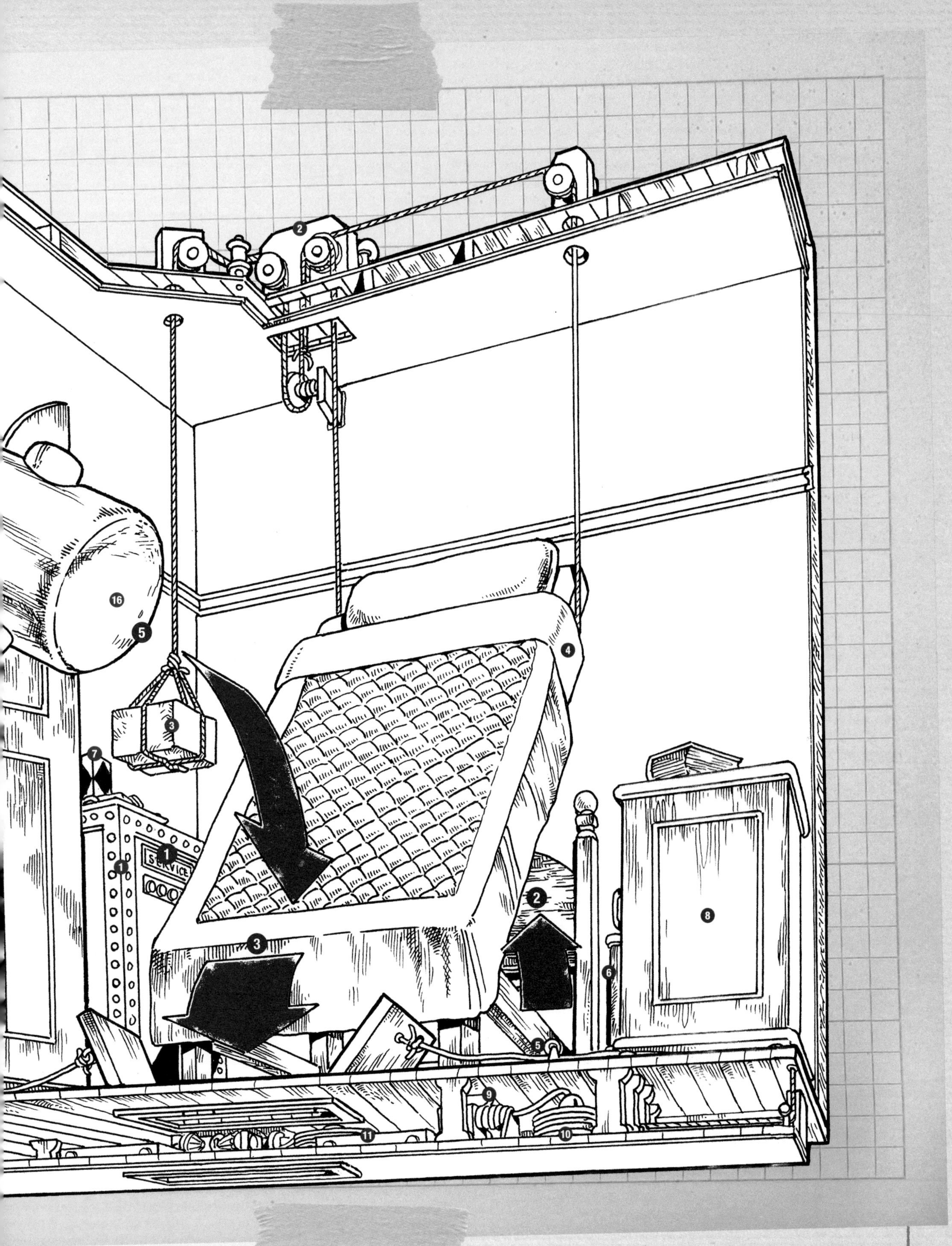
SERVICE
FOLIO

SUB HEADING

CUTAWAY HERE

Auto Dresser

BULLET LIST

6. The mallet 'assists' Wallace through the floor hatch and he lands on a chair at the dining table below.
7. The slipper deployment device puts Wallace's slippers on his feet.
8. The Autodresser puts on Wallace's trousers, followed by his tank top.
9. Finally, Wallace's shirt sleeves are put on by the ceiling-mounted overhead auto-dressing device.

❶ Activated Assistance Lever.

❷ Dining room table and tablecloth.

❸ Slipper deployment device.

❹ Hydraulic slipper deployment rams.

❺ Slipper deployment motor.

❻ Auto slipper placement grabs.

❼ Trouser holder bows place trousers over Wallace's legs.

❽ Auto Dresser.

❾ Auto Dresser control box.

❿ Shirt sleeve deployment grabs.

⓫ Fully articulated dressing arms.

⓬ Auto-dressing positioning rams.

⓭ Overhead auto-dressing device.

⓮ Mind Manipulation-O-Matic control console (concealed below table top).

⓯ Nest of tables and plant.

⓰ Door to kitchen.

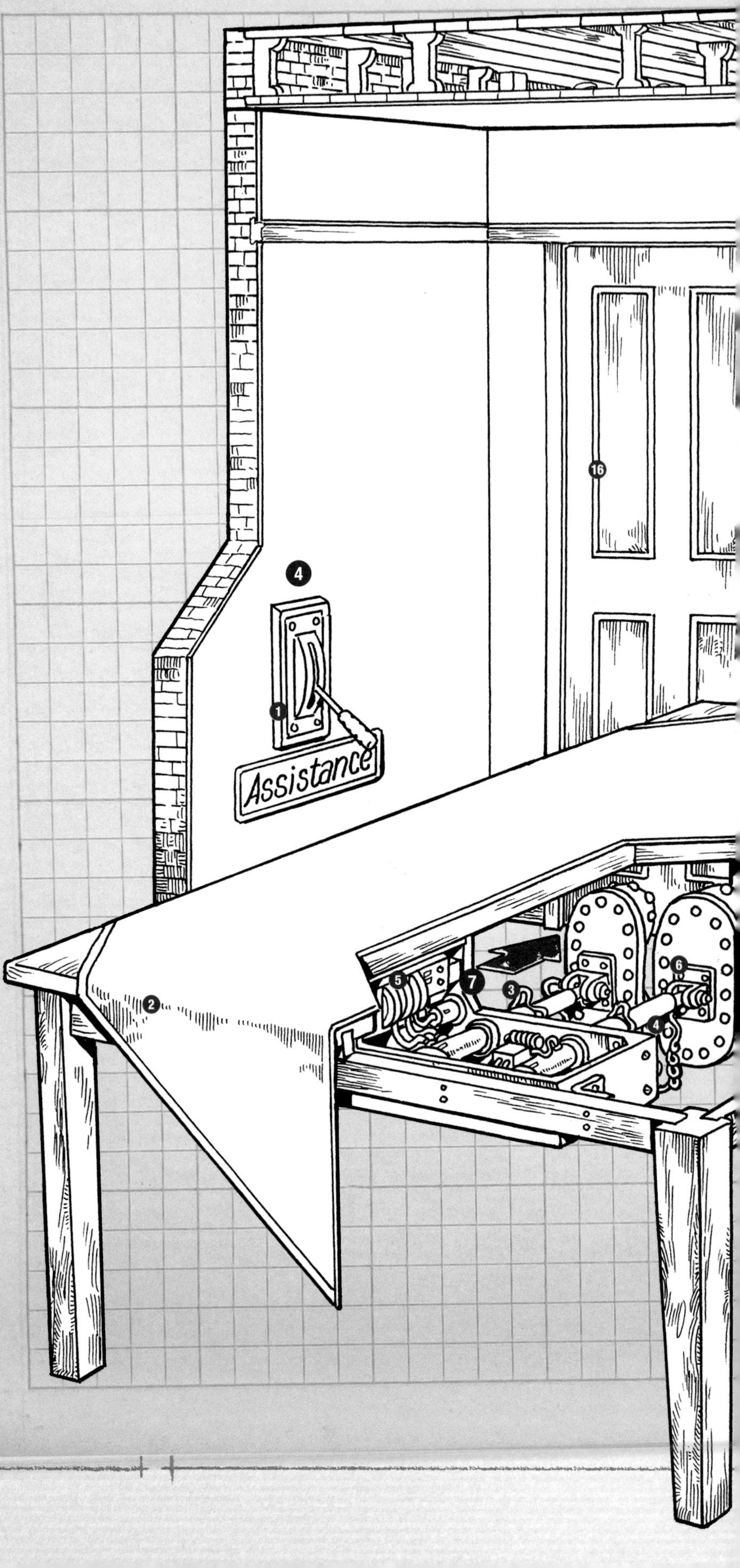

4
16
1
Assistance
2
5
7
3
6
4

FOLIO

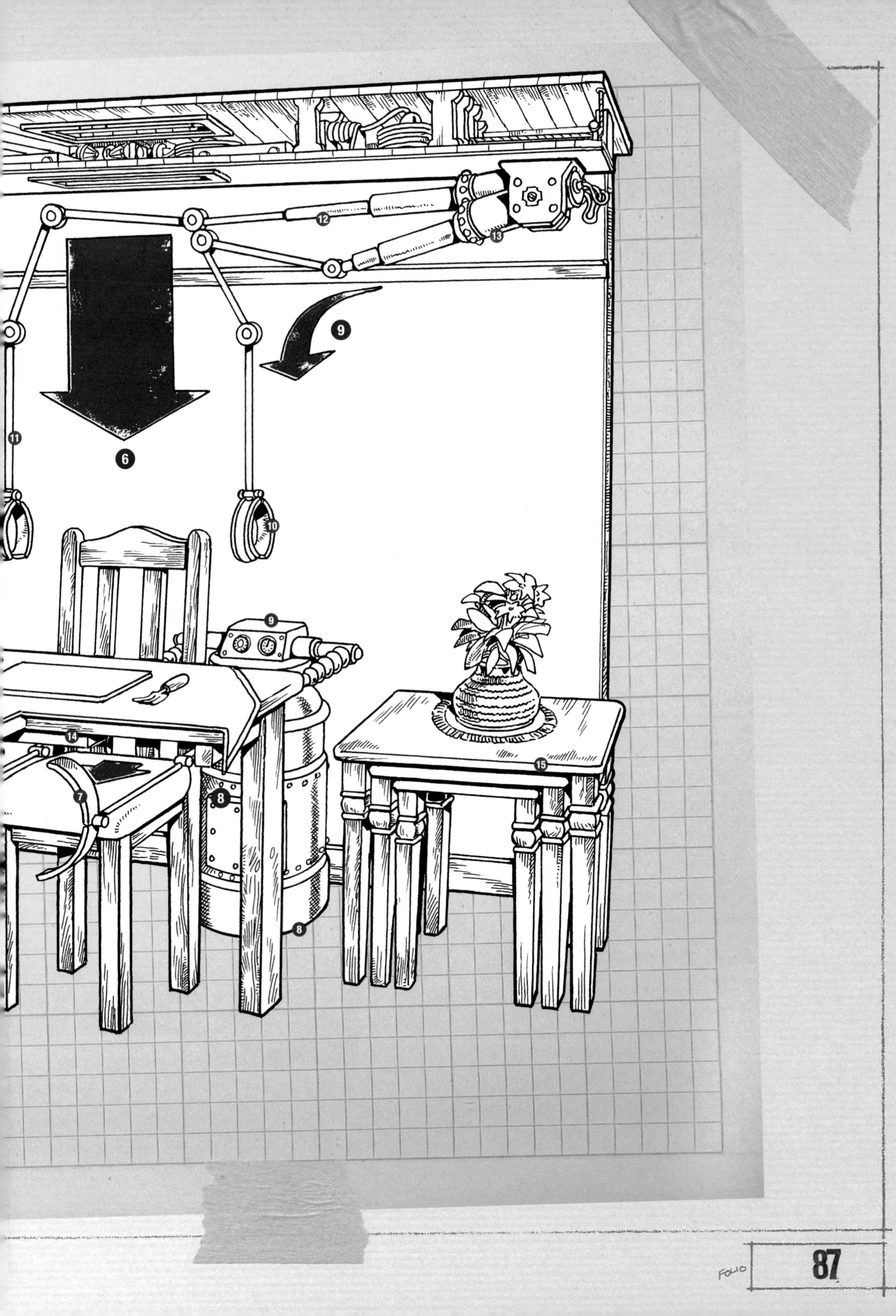
12
13
9
6
11
10
9
14
7
8
8
15

MAIN HEADING

MAIN PICTURE

PIE LAUNCHER

SUB HEADING

Contents

CONTENTS LIST

PAGE NO

SUB HEADING

General description

BODY COPY

DROP CAP

Wallace and Gromit's latest venture, WAG's Pies Ltd is doing a roaring trade, supplying hot pies to hungry football supporters. So much so, in fact, that Wallace decides to mobilise his latest invention: the Pie Launcher.

Hot pies from the WAG's Pies stall are loaded into two vertical stacking frames by an automated pincer mechanism. The frames are then lowered via telescopic arms to a position just above the Pie Launcher, which rises from the floor on elevation-adjusting supports into the firing position.

The Pie Launcher itself consists of a domed turret, inside of which is a sophisticated auto-fire pie-launching mechanism and associated targeting apparatus. The operator's seat is carried to the turret on a telescopic arm, entering via a hinged access hatch. Once the operator and seat are in position, the telescopic arm retracts, the access hatch closes and firing can commence.

Pies are released from the stacking frames and loaded into the barrel, one at a time, via two loading slides (one on each side of the turret). Before the pie enters the barrel, its foil dish is removed ready for discharge through one of two outlets located either side of the barrel. Firing is by means of a coil spring and shaped plunger, which propel the pie up and out of the barrel towards its target customer. The barrel is reloaded automatically from each loading slide alternately.

A range-finding telescopic gunsight is mounted on a tubular support beam fixed behind the operator. Targeting angle and elevation are controlled by the operator via a system of gears and chains, and actuated by a mains-powered electric motor installed behind the operator's seat.

Unfortunately, the auto-firing mechanism is liable to sticking, resulting in the rapid discharge of the entire supply of pies in both stacking frames.

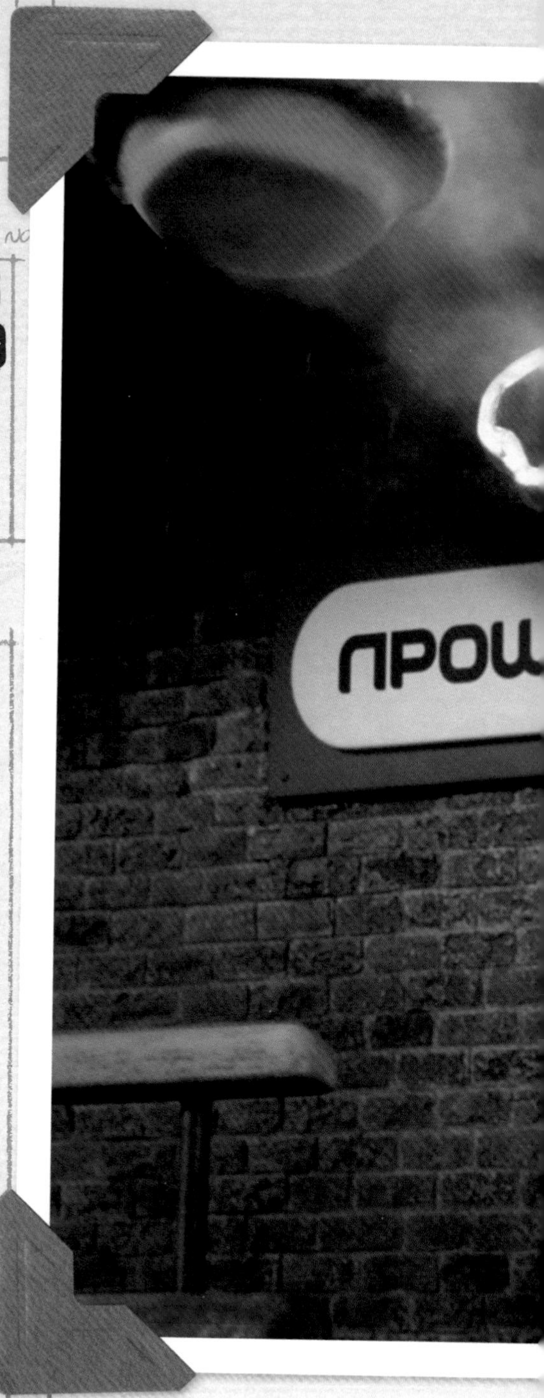

FOLIO

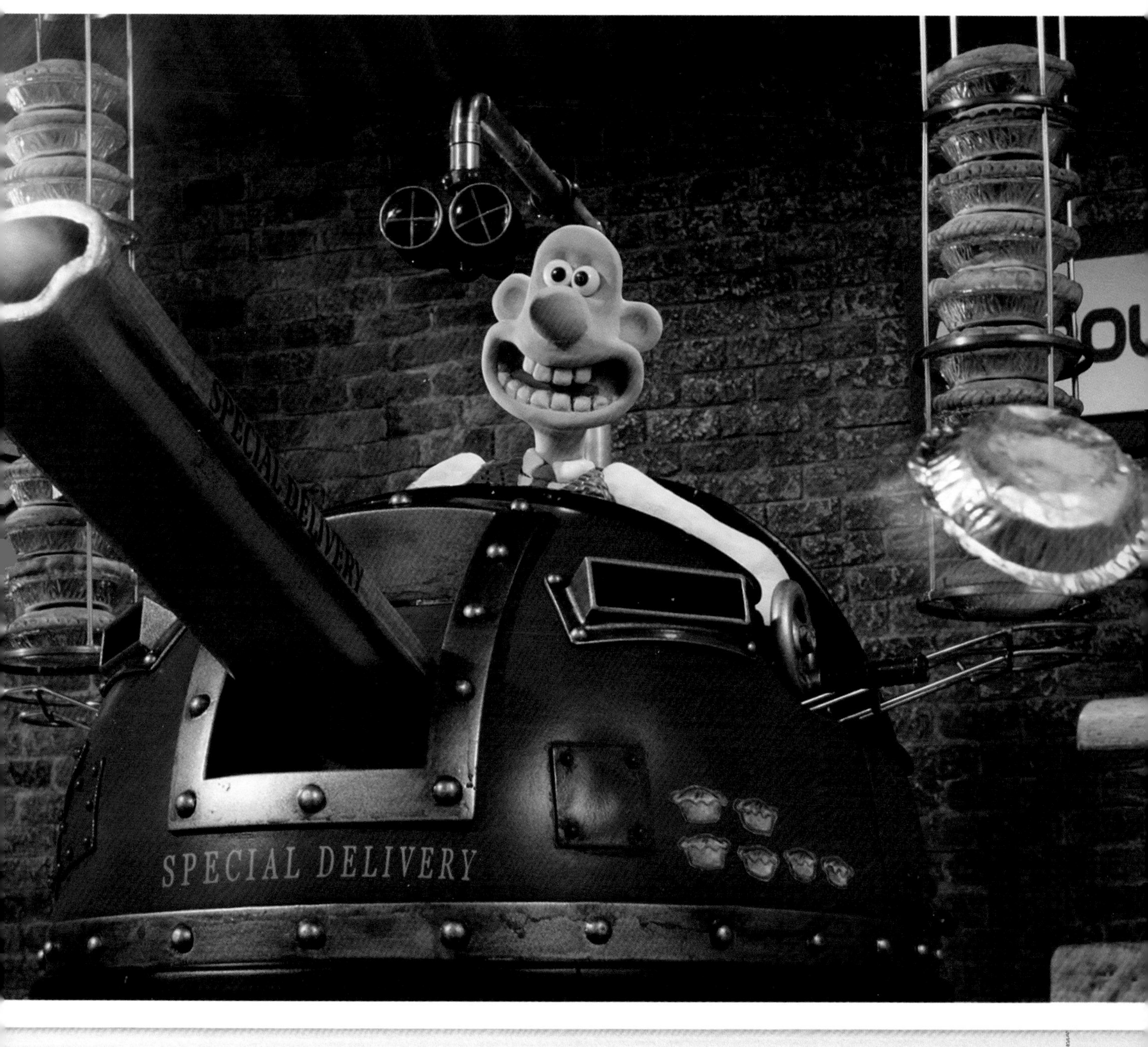
SPECIAL DELIVERY
SPECIAL DELIVERY

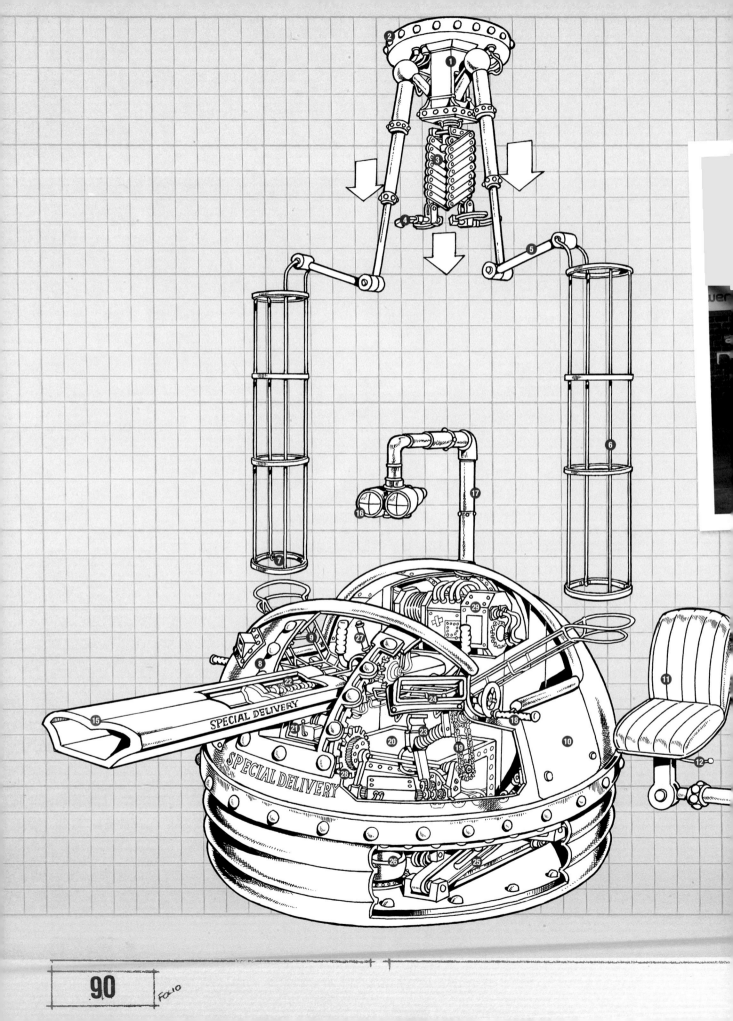

SPECIAL DELIVERY

SPECIAL DELIVERY

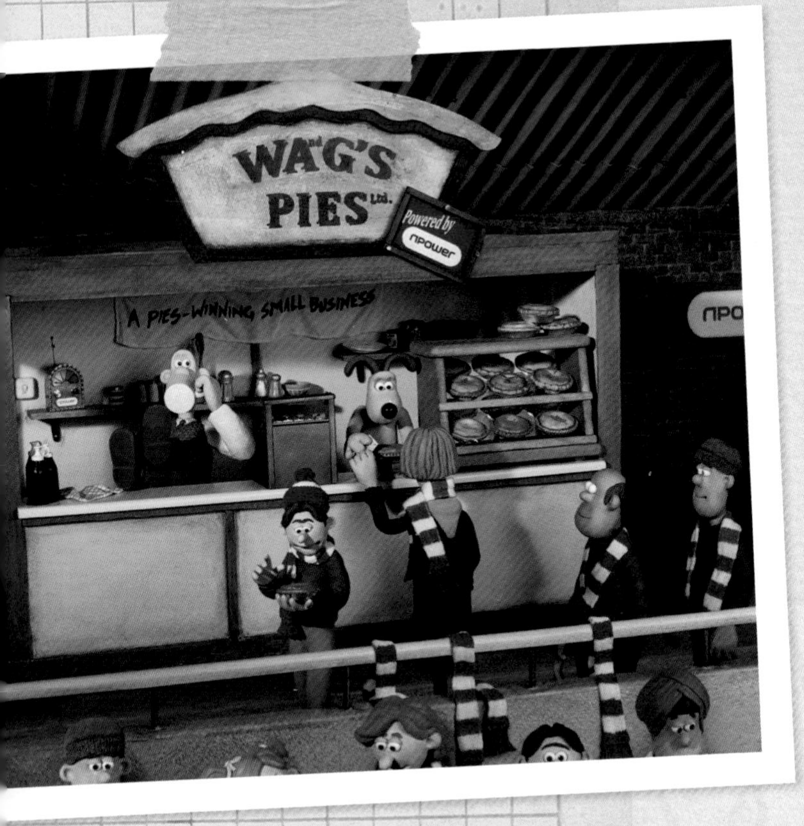
WAG'S
PIES Ltd.
Powered by
npower
A PIES-WINNING SMALL BUSINESS

Pie Launcher

1. Pie-stacking frame motor enclosure and release timer.
2. Roof attachment plate.
3. Pie-loading scissor arms.
4. Pie-loading pincers.
5. Pie-stacking frame telescopic positioning arms.
6. Pie-stacking frame (maximum capacity 18 pies).
7. Pie-release hooks, connected to release timer.
8. Pie Launcher turret.
9. Pie loading slide.
10. Gun turret access hatch.
11. Pie Launcher operator's seat.
12. Under-seat starting handle begins Wallace's entry to turret.
13. Telescopic access arm.
14. Access arm motor.
15. Pie-shaped discharge gun barrel.
16. Range-finding telescopic gunsight.
17. Gunsight tubular support beam.
18. Gun barrel elevation control handle.
19. Gun barrel elevation control gearing chains.
20. Operator's seat platform.
21. Pie barrel loading regulator and timer.
22. Pie launching coil spring.
23. Spring-operated foil dish removal device.
24. Foil dish discharge outlet.
25. Turret elevation-adjusting supports.
26. Turret rotation gearing and telescopic central support column.
27. Pie firing trigger (with automatic reload).
28. Pie Launcher elevation gears.
29. Mains-powered motor controls all functions.

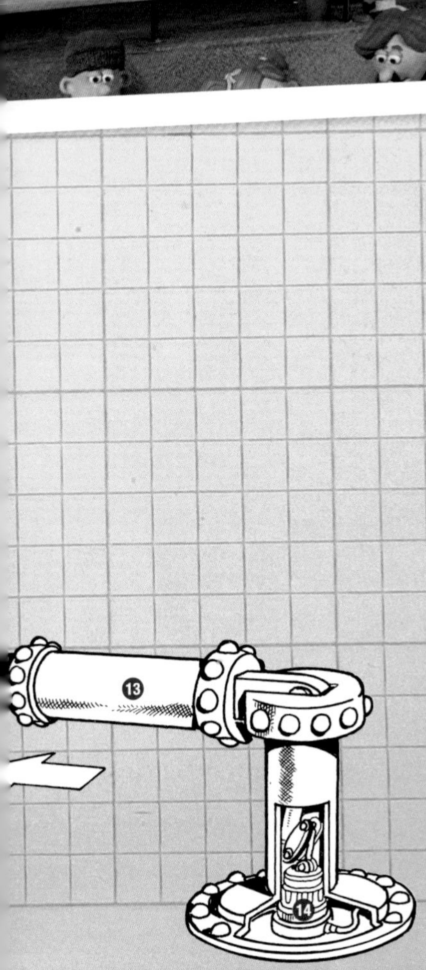
13
14

MAIN HEADING

WALLACE VISION

SUB HEADING

Contents

CONTENTS LIST PAGE NO.

SUB HEADING

General description

DROP CAP BODY COPY

Here is an invention that heralds a new dawn in home entertainment and one that might soon be seen in living rooms up and down the country. The Wallace Vision combines many television sets and video monitors (31 in total) to form a single tall and wide 'TV wall'. The resulting 'wide-screen' viewing experience is very large, very loud and totally immersive for the viewer.

While the sheer bulk of the Wallace Vision is impressive, the true ingenuity is found in the video signal distribution box, which, although large itself, fits snugly behind the TV wall. This is the heart of the machine and is responsible for receiving the primary broadcast signal (via the primary broadcast receiving antenna) and distributing it to all 31 TVs and video monitors. The video signal distribution box can either send different channels to individual screens, the same channel to all 31 screens, or take one channel and 'tile' it across the entire TV wall. The result created by this tiling effect is truly magnificent to behold, and even a little intimidating for novice users.

One of the key features of the TV wall is its modularity. If a particular TV set or monitor develops a fault, it can be simply replaced by another (of the same size, smaller or larger). Small screens can be upgraded to larger ones over time, and the TV wall can be expanded by adding further screens and connecting them to unused aerial lead outputs on the video signal distribution box.

If there is one drawback of the Wallace Vision then it is that the 31 television sets and monitors (some of them quite old and inefficient) together with the video signal distribution box consume a vast amount of power. Therefore, electricity is provided by a dedicated generator, which is positioned behind the TV wall, and built into the base of the generator is a necessarily large heat sink and cooling fan.

MAIN PICTURE

FOLIO

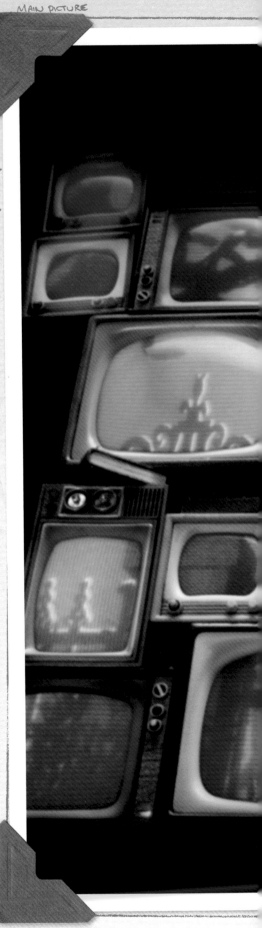

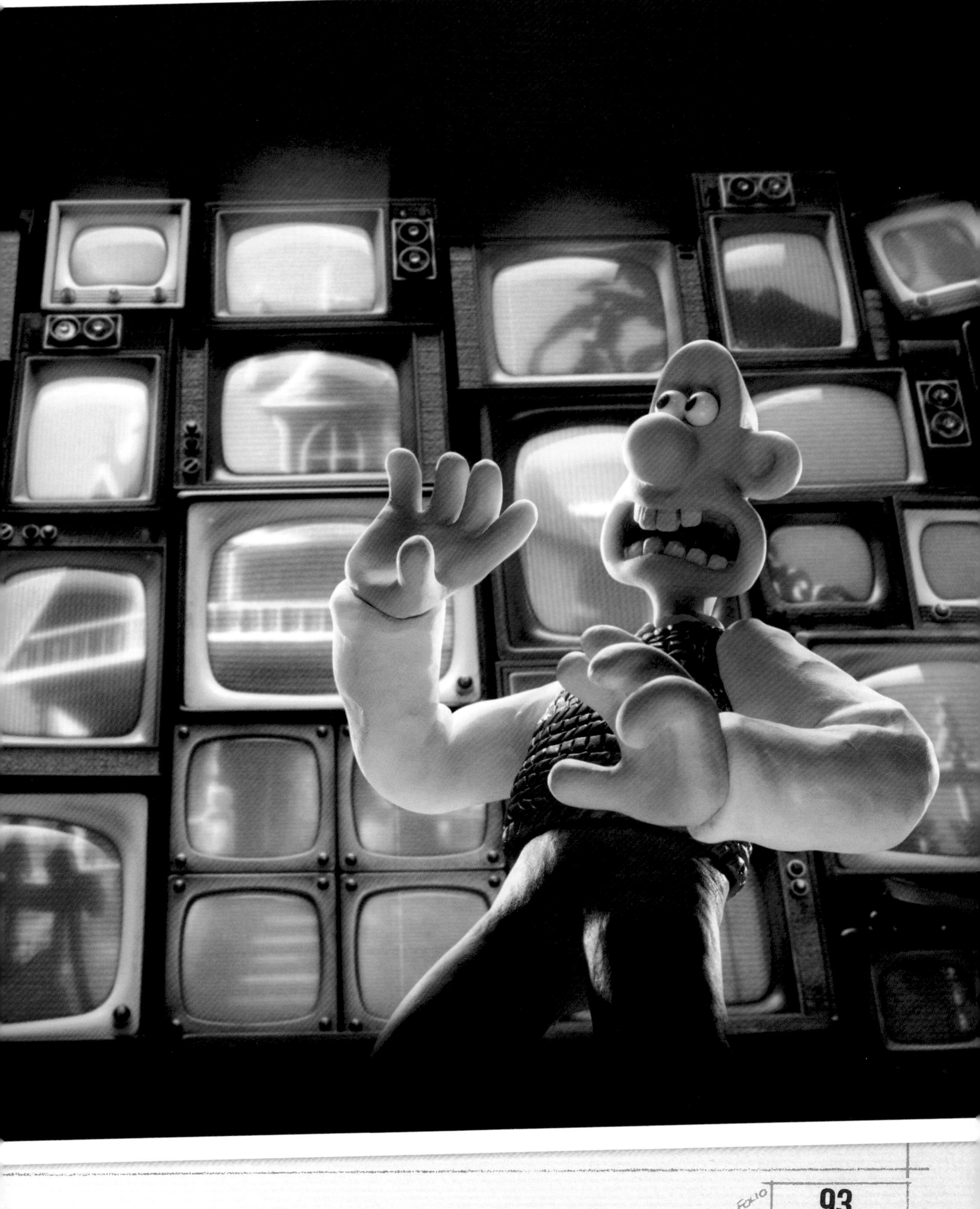

SUB HEADING

Wallace Vision

BULLET LIST

1. Video signal distribution box.
2. One of three multi-plug power distribution points linking television sets to generator.
3. Primary broadcast receiving antenna.
4. Aerial lead connectors.
5. Electricity generator provides ample power for all 31 television sets.
6. Generator cooling fan.
7. Individual TV antennae enable some televisions to display channels different to the main video feed from the video signal distribution box.
8. More aerial lead connectors.
9. Upside-down TV for better fitting.
10. Television support crook.
11. Books provide handy additional support in awkward gaps between television sets.
12. Strengthened coffee table provides support for seven televisions and four video monitors.
13. Set of four video monitors.
14. Anode.
15. Cathode.
16. Steering coils create magnetic fields to which the electron gun responds.
17. Electron gun.
18. Conductive tube coating.
19. Shadow mask.
20. Phosphor-coated screen.
21. Glass screen.
22. Cathode ray tube (CRT).
23. TV control electronics.

9
10
11

FOLIO

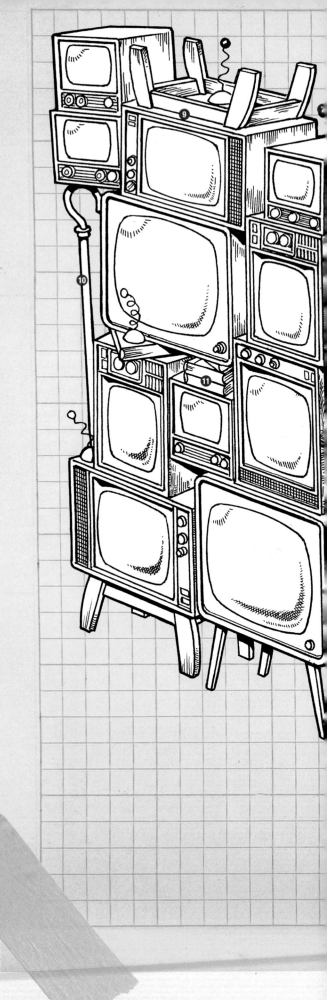

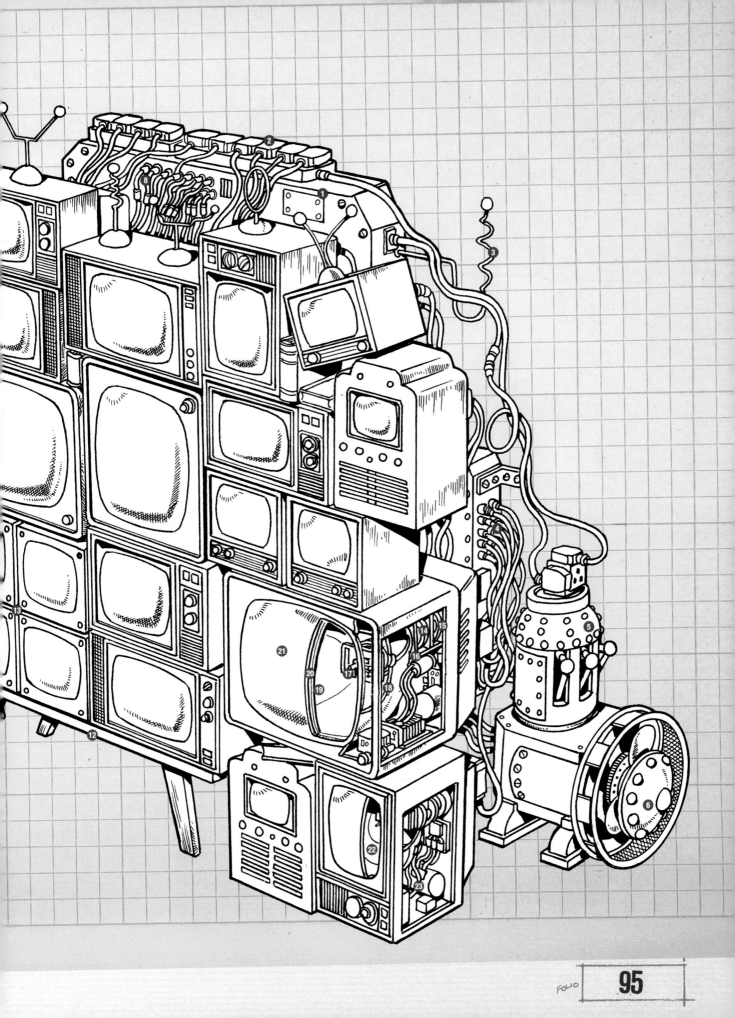

Wallace & Gromit

HAVE YOU SEEN OUR FIRST BOOK?

Packed with even more cracking contraptions

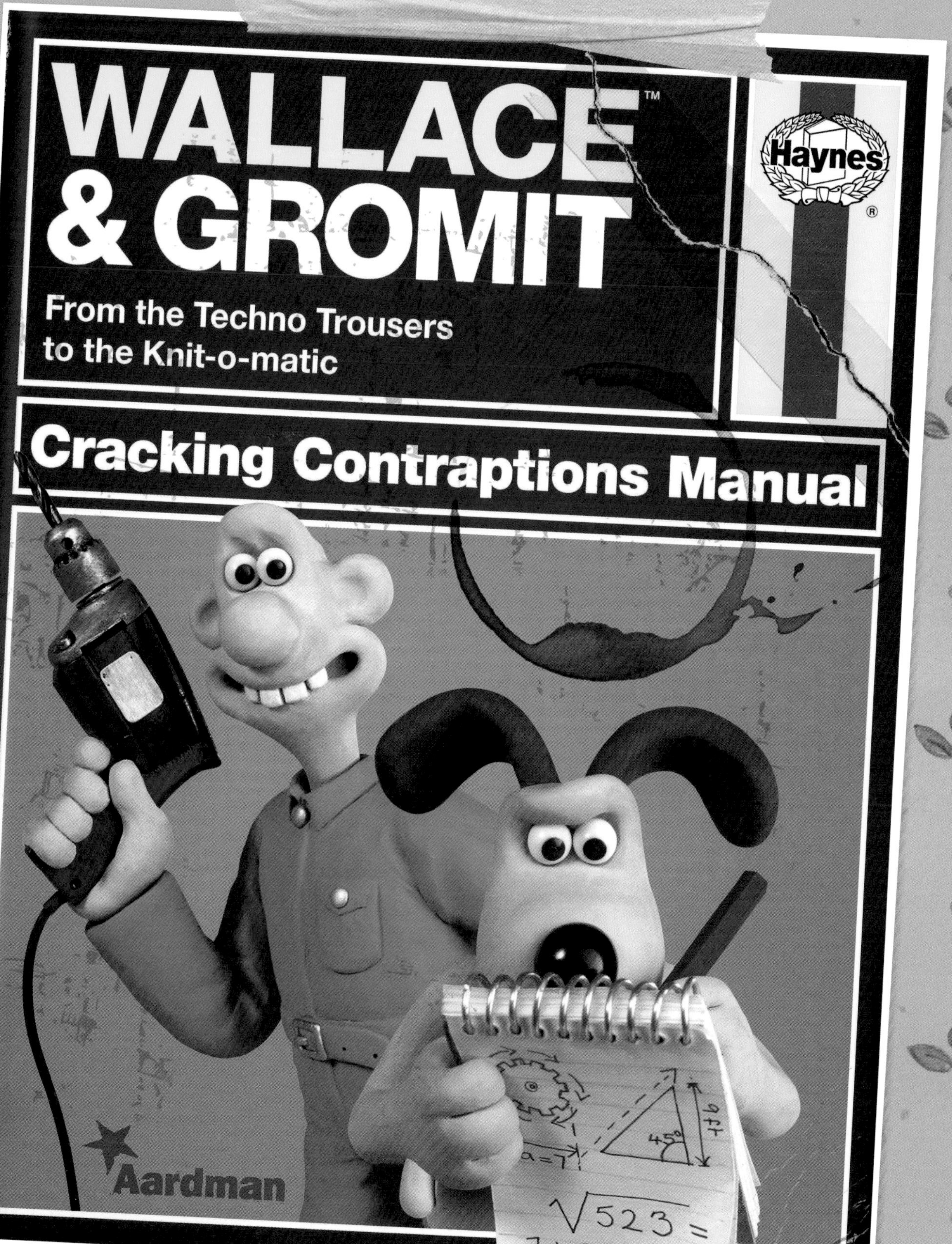
WALLACE™
& GROMIT
From the Techno Trousers
to the Knit-o-matic
Haynes
Cracking Contraptions Manual
45°
a=7
√523 =
Aardman

ACKNOWLEDGEMENTS

Special thanks are due to a small number of people
who have contributed to this book. Roughly in order of
appearance then: the inimitable Graham Bleathman for
again supplying such a splendid collection of cutaway
drawings, Lee Parsons for another top-drawer design job,
Jess Houston, Merlin Crossingham, Tristan Davies, Neil
Warwick and Kathryn Bramwell at Aardman for all their
support and assistance throughout, and finally Wallace,
Gromit and their Pronto Print machine, without which
this book just wouldn't be the same.

PICTURE CREDITS

All drawings are by Graham Bleathman. All other images
are courtesy of Aardman Animations.